letters to
Sarah

letters to Sarah

A CHILD LOST FOREVER, A MOTHER'S GRIEF
AND A LOVE THAT WILL NEVER DIE

SARA PAYNE

WITH

LINDA WATSON-BROWN

JOHN BLAKE

Published by John Blake Publishing,
3 Bramber Court, 2 Bramber Road,
London W14 9PB, England

www.johnblakebooks.com

www.facebook.com/johnblakebooks **f**
twitter.com/jblakebooks **t**

First published in paperback in 2017

ISBN: 978-1-78606-447-9

                                     2017

The right of Sam Payne and Linda Watson-Brown to be identified as the authors
of this work has been asserted by them in accordance with the Copyright,
Designs and Patents Act 1988.

Papers used by John Blake Publishing are natural, recyclable products made from
wood grown in sustainable forests. The manufacturing processes conform to the
environmental regulations of the country of origin.

Every attempt has been made to contact the relevant copyright-holders,
but some were unobtainable. We would be grateful if the appropriate
people could contact us.

John Blake Publishing is an imprint of Bonnier Publishing
www.bonnierpublishing.co.uk

For Mole and for Shy – always there, always beside
me on the journey

And for my beautiful children – you keep
me sane . . . almost!

Contents

Sarah — and Sara

On Saturday, 1 July 2000, eight-year-old Sarah Payne was playing with her two brothers and sister near the home of her grand-parents in West Sussex. The children argued and Sarah wandered off at around 8pm on that summer's eve. No one saw her again. Sara Payne reported her missing daughter and local emergency service teams, combined with police, searched all night, with no success.

By the next day, more than fifty officers and almost one hundred volunteers undertook a fingertip search of the area. Sarah's brother Lee revealed that he saw a white van and a grinning man in the lane where she would have walked. That day, a known paedophile called Roy Whiting, then aged forty-one, was arrested but later released on bail.

On the Monday, Sara and Michael Payne made their first televised appeal for the return of their little girl — it was to be one of many. The country immediately rallied to the side of the distraught couple, and in particular reached out to Sara, who spoke to all parents as she begged *for her daughter to come home. It was on that day that the police first admitted that Sarah could have been taken by a stranger. Two days later, they staged an identity parade, which included Whiting, but were forced to release him again on bail, this time pending further inquiries.*

It turned into a horrific waiting game. As the days passed, everyone's worst fears were turning into the most likely reality. By 6 July, every police force in the UK was involved in the hunt for Sarah, but the actual search was scaled down so that the inquiry could focus on specific leads. The next day, the police staged a reconstruction of the little girl's last-known movements in an attempt to jog the memory of anyone who might have seen her. This resulted in more than 3,000 calls from the public. Roadblocks were set up and motorists quizzed to see if anyone else recalled the white van seen by thirteen-year-old Lee. Along with his eleven-year-old brother Luke, and six-year-old sister Charlotte, Lee helped the police all he could, but there was not the swift resolution hoped for by the whole nation. There soon followed another emotional televised appeal, but the search entered a second week amid fears of how it might end.

The entire country waited and the story spread across the world. Each news bulletin led with updates and Sarah Payne was fast becoming recognised by everyone, but on 13 July, her mother was told to prepare for the worst. The emphasis of the inquiry had shifted and it became unlikely that Sarah would be found safe and well. Two days later, the whole family returned to the beach where the children had been playing just before Sarah disappeared, but any hope they might have had was soon shattered when, on the Monday, police found a body.

On Tuesday, 18 July, they confirmed that it was indeed Sarah and opened a murder investigation.

Sarah — and Sara

At the end of July, Roy Whiting was again arrested and again released on police bail. But it was not until after a further Crimewatch appeal on BBC1 in January 2001 that he was finally charged with Sarah's murder. On 12 December 2001, he was found guilty of abducting and murdering little Sarah, and jailed for life.

Over those eighteen months, Sara Payne never rested. Knowing that her child had been the victim of a convicted paedophile made her convinced that there needed to be a change in the law so that ordinary people could find out when there was an offender living nearby. It transpired that Whiting had a 1995 conviction for sexually assaulting another young girl, and it was this knowledge that finally convinced Sara there should be new legislation to, hopefully, prevent the same thing ever happening again. Sara fought for a version of Megan's Law, an American statute whereby communities were told the whereabouts of known paedophiles. Sarah's Law would be a testament to the little girl who had touched the hearts of a nation — and it was to be the campaign that continued to endear her mother to everyone.

Sara Payne told her story in the aftermath of those early events, but hers is a tale that never ends. With a daughter whose name is still a byword for victims' rights and a character that endeared her to a nation, now is the time for her to tell exactly what happened in the years that followed — and how she has survived every parent's worst nightmare.

Prologue

It has been seventeen years since you went missing, Sarah. It has been twenty-five years since you were born. There have been too many Christmases without you.

So, why now? Why am I telling everyone these things now? Has something happened?

Everything has happened, and nothing has happened.

I would love to be able to say that, after a very specific amount of time, you get over it. If you wait a year, or a decade, or any other amount of time, you will wake up one day and it won't feel so raw, it won't hurt as much. But I'd be lying.

It's always there . . .

. . . even when it isn't.

I'll always be your mum, but I'll also always be the mother of murdered schoolgirl, Sarah Payne. I stand with every other bereaved parent when I say this: you can't put a time limit on grief.

I wanted to write this book at a time when there was no anniversary because for me every day is an anniversary – another day without you, but another day I've survived. Every parent who has lost a child will understand that. They will know what I mean when I say that every day is as bad as the rest, has the potential to be as good as the rest. Dates do matter – but it's the loss that really counts.

There are testaments to you, my beautiful girl, everywhere: amongst the public, in legislation, online, in hearts and minds and memories. I don't need a specific date to think about you and I don't need to be given permission to say what I need to say – I have moved on, princess, I have moved on. That doesn't mean I've forgotten or that I don't care, but, for so long, I was little more than the woman defined by what was done to my child. Now, I have found the courage to say, *this is who I am.*

I am more than that, more than what happened, and the best testament I can give you is that I have lived my life. At times, it was almost unbearable – but there has been happiness and love and laughter and joy along the way, and I won't apologise for that.

Do you understand?

I'm holding back a little even as I write this because I know people will judge – they will say that they could never get past it; those people were the ones who said they would never cope if it happened to them. I always felt they were the most judgemental of all – by saying they would never have been able to cope, it was almost as if they were condemning me for still being here. Their grief would have been bigger; their hearts would have shattered more. The truth is, I *had* to cope. Not just for the others, but for you. If I had broken into a million pieces, who would have remembered you in the way I did? No one has the memories of a mother, no one can make you live again in the way I can.

You have stayed in my heart every day since you were taken from me; nothing anyone could ever do could change that. Our family has been through so much, but we have survived, just as your memory has survived. Before you left, I could never imagine you as an adult. I just couldn't see you ever getting beyond the age where you were everyone's little princess. I thought, for some reason, I didn't have the imagination, although I'd had it with all the others. It wasn't some sort of psychic vision, it just 'was'. So many things have had to be accepted for what they are, but I believe everything happens for a reason.

There have been dark days, dark nights, dark times when to me that reason has been hidden. What could possibly justify what happened to you? How could the world possibly be a better place without you in it? I've had to try and unpack that, Sarah. I've had to come to terms with you not being here, but life going on.

Every time something happens, on the news or in the family, I want you to share it. And you do. I tell you everything. I wish there were only good things to tell, but, more than many, our family knows that isn't how life works. So, I've tried to make sense of it. To take it all apart and put it back together again in a way that fits this broken world. There have been times when nothing has worked, and other times when everything makes sense.

But, I knew one thing throughout it all.

I had to give you a legacy and I did.

I'm your legacy, Sarah.

It's the wrong way round, but it's how the cards have fallen.

Here's the rest of your story, princess – be proud. xx

Author's note

I have spent so much time talking to Sarah – telling her things, keeping her up to date on all our lives – I have never stopped talking to her really. But it's always been between us, until now. It was only recently that I looked back and realised just how much of life had happened since she left us – some things seem like yesterday, but when I think about it more closely, years have gone by. So, these are all those little things and big things and everything-in-between words put together. These are the letters I wanted to send my daughter, the letters she'll never read, but the letters I needed to write.

Summer 2017

DEAR SARAH —

It's true that you always loved stories — and I did too. We both loved them when we were little girls, then when you were my little girl. You'd curl up in my arms, your soft hair tickling my face; my gorgeous eight-year-old, my first daughter. There were princesses and knights, dragons and castles, fairy tales and adventures. I would say that it was bedtime, and you would beg for *just one more*, and I would always give in.

I have a story to tell you now, Sarah. It will be hard to read in parts, but please stay with me as it unfolds, because who knows? There may be a happy ending — we all need to remember that there is always the hope of one of those. Are you ready?

Once upon a time, there was a little girl. On a warm summer's day, close to her granny's house, the little girl was playing with her brothers and sister. They had all begged to play on the beach together, with the early evening sun casting a golden glow over everyone and everything. They wanted to squeeze as much fun as they could out of the long summer days – they wanted to be children for as long as possible. The little girl had never, ever been left alone. Always she had been surrounded by the affection of her family, by their big, noisy love that kept her protected at all times. She wouldn't be alone this time either – her two big brothers and her younger sister would be there too. So, a little bit of summer freedom was granted. Her mummy wasn't too far away, and her daddy was nearby too.

But *not too far away* was still *too far away*. And when the bad man came and took the little girl, *nearby* didn't matter.

Once upon a time, there was a woman whose little girl was taken from her. Everyone in the kingdom knew that the little girl had disappeared and they looked for her if they could. If they couldn't look, they listened for stories and prayed that she had been found. It was as if the whole kingdom was on pause that summer. Everyone wondered the same thing – where was the little girl and when would she come home?

As the days passed, the questions changed and the hope faded. People stopped asking when the little girl would come home; they started to ask when she would be found. And when they asked that question, the hope slipped from their voices. Stories began to circulate about the bad man. The little girl's brother had seen a van near to where his sister disappeared. He had seen a man with broken teeth and the sneering look of a wolf, who had broken into the story and changed the ending forever. The people looking for the little girl started to speak more about the man and what he might have done; they seemed to forget their plans to welcome the child home. The little girl's mummy stayed strong. She asked for help and she made sure that no one forgot about her daughter – but, one day, it was hard to stay strong any more.

One day, everyone realised the little girl would never come home. They were all very sad and when they finally found the bad man who had taken the little girl, they got very angry.

The little girl's mummy was very sad and very angry too. She knew that it would be easier to let her own heart break, because hearts often want to do that when the world doesn't make sense any more. However, as she stood and looked at the two paths ahead of her, she didn't choose the easy one of heartbreak, she chose the much harder path – the path with thorns and darkness and struggle; she chose the path of survival.

I want to tell you the story of my journey down that path, Sarah. I want to tell you of how the bad man, the bad wolf, the bad things, didn't win: you did. Your heart and softness and wonder were stronger than any of the terrible things that came to light that summer. You gave the world so much, even although you were taken from us. I need to tell you the rest of your story now, princess. Are you listening?

Then let's begin . . . xx

2000

When I have told my story before, to other people, when I told it at the start, I think there was an element of presenting it in a certain way. I'm not alone in that — we all have a version of our lives that we share with the world, and while I wasn't lying about how your dad and I were with each other, I did perhaps keep out some of the details. Maybe I was looking through rose-tinted glasses, maybe I was just trying to find something good in life — no one could blame me for that, I hope; I needed something. We all became public property so quickly, Sarah — no one could ever prepare themselves for what happened to us, but I think the way in which the public took you, and us, to their hearts made me feel that I had to give them something back.

11

You were our little girl and you had been taken from us in the most terrible way. I needed to feel that we could survive it. It's funny to talk about this with you – I wonder what you would have asked me as you got older? You knew a lot of our story, but not all of it was quite as I presented it to the rest of the world. I'm sitting here, watching an old year fade into a new one, and thinking you are the only person I can talk to about all of this, even though you aren't even here any longer. I certainly can't talk to your dad about it. Michael is the very person who should be sharing all of this, but losing you . . . it's pushed us apart, not brought us together. But there were wonderful times, there really were.

Ours was a young love. Your dad and I were little more than children ourselves when we got together, but we built a family and we both loved our children with all our hearts. We loved all of you with every breath in our bodies. I think people have seen how strong we are as a family now, but they don't see everything. I was determined to keep it together, to keep my marriage and my family together, when you were taken from us all, but the truth was, we weren't the perfect little team we made out. We had money worries for a start. We drank too much. We stumbled from day to day a lot of the time, never really planning, never really being proper grown-ups. Both of us were in menial jobs and it had been a struggle for a while. Our main concern was putting food on the table and as long as we did that, I felt we were coping, but we did make mistakes along the way.

I had always wanted a big family; it was the most natural set-up in the world to me. Having lots of children was a given. I was young – eighteen – when I had my first baby, your first big brother Lee, and I had been protected all my life. I wanted a family of my own, and I got one. I wanted a baby while I was still young, and I got one. My own parents had given me and my siblings such a strong foundation; everything had always worked out in my life – I simply didn't have any reason to believe it would ever be any different. Nothing had happened in my life to make me think the world wasn't a good place.

I suppose I'm telling you these things now because I'm worried that it all might slip away. You shouldn't have to say goodbye to your own child, no one should ever have to go through that, but it's done, it's happened, and I feel like I have to keep this connection to you, my darling, and telling you these things helps. You would have just absorbed it all had you still been with us. As you grew, you would look at our family and realise how we worked, and see the bits that didn't work. You would have just taken it all on board naturally, whereas now I feel that I have to make sure that you understand it all. I do feel as if you're still with me, Sarah, and I want you to stay with me.

Your grandad was a calm man, your nan a very positive person, and everything was family-focused – you must remember they were like that, because they were still the same when we had you. We weren't particularly ambitious, despite the fact that Mum was from a very middle-class, well-spoken background – all any of us wanted was the same life that we'd had ourselves. Your nan was a great role model for me; yes, she was strict – and I sometimes wished I was able to be that way with you lot – but she was supportive and generous too. We were close, always. I was the fifth child but I never felt that I was loved any less, or that they were a bit dulled by it all by the time I came along. I was lucky to have them. I think I would say, to turn an old phrase around, we knew the value of everything and the cost of nothing. My mum and dad were always keen to make us feel that people mattered, not things. They saw the goodness in the world and they never judged anyone for what they had, or what they didn't have. I absorbed all of that and I hope that I'll always carry the values they gave me, and that I'll be able to pass them on to my own children. Isn't it funny, darling; I still think that you will be your own, kind, wonderful self wherever you are now. I'm not religious, you know that, but I can't bear to think you've just gone. I feel you everywhere, and I feel that your kindness is still around.

When I settled down with your dad, it wasn't the dream life I had anticipated. There was love, and there were babies, but ours was a difficult relationship. We were too young and there was too much conflict. I was feisty – and so was he. We clashed – we clashed a lot. But . . . I wonder . . . am I even telling the full story there? Was that all it was? Did we just 'clash'?

We were toxic.

That's the truth of it.

We had grown up together but changed into different people. Your dad was a hard worker but he had no dreams and never really fulfilled his potential – in fact, I don't know if he even thought he had any potential. Not long after Lee arrived, there was Luke. Then there was you, then was along came Charlotte. I had my big, messy family, but it wasn't a storybook life. All of you, you were all I ever wanted, but our life wasn't perfect. There wasn't enough money, there was too much drinking ... There was a lot of love, but there was a lot of fighting too. We did our best for you kids, but maybe we didn't do our best for each other.

By the time you were taken, princess, there were problems, but losing a child in that way changes everything. We had to be together for your brothers and sister, and for the fight to try and get you back. Dad was uncomfortable with that from the start, he was uncomfortable with the way we had to fight. He hated the media attention but I knew it was a necessary evil. I was in the driving seat, I admit it – I felt from the start that we needed the media on our side. At the start, I thought you might still be out there. I had to believe we could get you home, and I needed every journalist in the country to get the message out. If there was the slightest chance my little girl could be found, I wanted every single person to know her face and her name so they could bring her home to me. I would have done anything. And I did – I did all that was asked of me, but I had no idea, even in the early days, that it was tearing your dad and me away from each other.

Letters to Sarah

As the days passed, I was aware of everything. There was no twenty-four-hour-a-day news coverage at that time, so bulletins were followed by the whole country at set times. People sat down to watch the 9 o'clock or 10 o'clock programmes, and it was here that they caught up on what was happening. Nor were the internet and social media anything like as widespread and as influential then as they are now. I was in the middle of it – we all were – and there was never a time when I found out anything new from those bulletins as the police and journalists were so good at keeping me up to date, but I still watched them all, I still listened to every word . . . just in case. Maybe there was a snippet that would help, a clue no one had told me about that would mean something to me; that would take me to you. It wasn't likely; I knew all of the people who made those stories and programmes, but I still hoped.

The first Christmas without you has been so strange, darling. I've put a barrier around me, quite deliberately. I've been trying to build a brick wall, I've been trying to feel numb – I feel everything and yet I feel so little. One minute I feel as cold as ice, as if nothing will ever touch me, then the next, I feel raw with emotion, as if every part of me is exposed to the world. I don't think anyone sees that because of the barrier I've put around me. I think the whole world believes I'm coping, that I'm some sort of superwoman for how I've got through this. I'm wrecked, that's the honest truth. Losing you, looking for you, knowing we'd never see you again, starting the campaign

… there's no guidebook on how to deal with any of that. Nothing to tell me how I should be, so I'm muddling through, being what I need to be for other people while my arms are aching from the loss of you, Sarah.

I've done nothing for the festive season this year, which will seem so odd to you because you know how much I love it, but a few friends have saved Christmas for us. They've rallied round and provided a tree, organised presents, reminded me ever so gently that I need to do something for the children I still have. If Michael and I had been left to our own devices, it would have been just another day. Every time I looked at the others, there was pain. You aren't here, but they are. I still have children, I can't concentrate so much on the one I don't have any more that I forget the ones who are still here. I'd let them down again – that was all I could think. I can't help but feel that I have put them all in the middle of everything. If I wasn't their mother, they would be protected from such things – but I *am* their mother and they're not protected at all. They have me and they don't have you, and their lives too will never be the same again. It's been so hard, Sarah – I haven't just lost you, I've been in danger of losing myself.

This year, I've become someone I don't recognise. I wonder what you would think of me? You would laugh, I bet – you would take it all in your stride, and tell me you love me. All of this would have been easier with you by my side, but it was only through the loss of you that I've had to do it all in the first place. I've done things I never imagined I was capable of. I've spoken to politicians, decision-makers – the ones with power, the ones who can change things for other children – and I've never flinched. I've had to do it; I've had to do it for you. I quickly realised that they had no idea, princess. Even the ones who came from normal, average backgrounds changed once they became politicians, and they forgot what real life was like. I've brought the barmaid to them and, to be honest, I'm quietly proud of that. They've all kept telling me that the changes I want to make will unleash vigilante attacks but I suspect that won't be the case at all; I've long believed the biggest problem amongst people is apathy. People would rather not do anything, preferring to live in ignorance rather than face problems. They won't take to the streets with pitchforks if they know a sex offender is living nearby, I know they won't. I just want them to have that knowledge, to be aware of any potential danger lurking nearby, and to challenge the horrendous culture of secrecy in our children's lives.

Now that Christmas is finally over, I know how much I want to keep talking to you. I want to tell you everything that has happened even though I'm sure you must know. Do you, or am I going mad? Do you know that I've learned to bury things better? I keep going back to that because it seems to be the key to everything. Is that what grieving people do? Is that what all lost mothers do? There must be a whole army of us out there – silent, invisible, hearts broken for the want of our children, but ignored because no one really wants to address that degree of loss, do they?

When it all happened, I didn't really want the world or the other kids to see what I truly felt, so I put up that brick wall. I hardened my heart – well, what was left of it. I was such a positive person until now – I can still fake a lot, but behind it all . . . I'm not even sure how I feel.

Your dad and I stopped talking almost as soon as you went missing, darling. We just couldn't connect emotionally, and we still can't. I feel as if he can't empathise with me. Isn't that the strangest thing? We should be a team, we should know exactly what the other one is thinking and feeling, but it's thrown us apart, not together.

We've lost each other.

Do you know what I need? What I've needed from him since this whole nightmare began? I've needed him to take the reins. The irony is, maybe I would never have actually allowed him to, but I needed him to *try*. He hated the press intrusion, he still does, but I've accepted that it's just a different world that I need to visit every so often.

Everyone judges us, I know that, but there has been so much kindness too. I don't think Dad sees the kindness, he just sees the people who behave badly, the ones who blame us for ever being apart from you. He hears the whispers that say it was our fault, that we brought it on ourselves, whereas I try to shrug it off. I know you were loved, I know this was a one-in-a-million chance; I know we have to try and stick together. He can't see any of that.

Letters to Sarah

As a child I was so loved, so pampered in a way, always thinking the world was a good place, and I still have the after-effects of that, no matter what has happened. I've disengaged. I'm *not myself* as people say. I could laugh at that. I have no idea who I am any more, but maybe *myself* will come back one day. I'm going to keep ploughing through, just in case, but I won't do it raw – I won't allow anyone in. There's Lee and Luke and Charlotte – they are everything to me. No one else even comes close. Does your dad understand that? I don't think so. I've buried you deep inside me, princess. I've buried you, and I still have three other children to love and look after – can he not do that for himself? Do I have to pick up the pieces for him too?

Sometimes though, I wonder if I'm being too harsh on him – he has his own demons. The more I think about it, the more I think it's the fear of people judging him that makes him the way he is. But all families are judged when something happens to one of their children. People need to distance themselves, comfort themselves that it will never happen to them, so they look to see if they can blame you in some way. Or sometimes people act as though something terrible that happens to someone else might be catching, so they avoid them. If you'd never been found, would we have been blamed more? Would people think we had done something awful to you? It doesn't bear thinking about, there is enough chatter as it is. Across the country, there has been support, tremendous support that I will always be grateful for, but, also, there will be voices who want to be nasty – not as many as the good people, but they have a disproportionate effect. I see it in their faces sometimes, Sarah. I see them thinking, *you weren't a good enough mother, you didn't protect her enough; this is your fault.* Some people hate us because of what was done to you, and your dad can't cope with that. I try not to listen; I try not to hear the whispers.

I was such an open and friendly person, but the whispers have changed me as much as losing you has done. I don't think local people understand that. They don't understand where the friendly barmaid has gone – they certainly don't know she's on automatic pilot most of the time.

Clever people tell me that I have post-traumatic stress disorder, and that this PTSD makes me feel as if I'm outside looking in. I certainly knew I was in shock. I was shell-shocked – that's what it is, isn't it? That's what PTSD really is, it's what soldiers coming back from battle feel, and my God, I've been through some battles this year. I feel as if the world is underwater, Sarah. Everything is muffled. I have no concept of time, nothing has any context. I'm exhausted, I never seem to sleep. And now, now I feel guilty I'm telling you all of this. You're just a little girl, you'll always be just a little girl, and I would never have confided in you like this if you were still here, so that makes me think I shouldn't be doing it now either. Who else do I have though, princess, who else is there for me?

Am I doing this right? My thoughts are all over the

place as I write to you. Maybe things will become clearer, maybe the grief will make sense one day. I'm a ghost in my own life, and sometimes that ghost is a foolish one. I still daydream that someone will come to the door and say it's all been a terrible mistake; that it wasn't you. Oh, the comfort when I have those moments! I want to slip inside them forever. But real life always comes back and you're still gone. This year has shown me so much, but the main thing is that I'm not ready to let you go. We'll keep this between us. I'll tell you who I am and you can watch over me while I do it.

And what will next year bring? Will we ever know the truth? Will we ever know what he, whatever type of man he turns out to be, did to you? I can't imagine it will ever end, and I can't imagine how I will ever feel normal again, whatever that means.

I love you, darling – please help me get through this. xx

2001

DARLING SARAH —

So much to talk to you about, so very much, princess.

We know who he is now — we knew from early this year.
We watched as TV showed it all again, we watched as the
police arrested him again, we watched as the police charged
him, and we watched as he finally went to court. I don't
want to name him even though I'll have to — I don't want
to give him any status at all really. The police always thought
it was him; they tried to find out whether he was involved
from the very early days, but now, finally, they know.

Dad is finding it hard to cope. Women and men are so
different in grief. His anger has taken him over but I won't
let it near me. I think that men are more violent in their
thought processes and he knows who he wants to 'get'. We

have a particular person to identify as the person who did this to our family, not an imaginary bogeyman, and your dad, as a man, wants to do something about that, about him. I don't want to feel that way and that's made me, in many ways, remove myself from Dad. I've had to; I've had to protect myself in any way I can.

We've waited all year for him, for the man who took you, to say something. He didn't – but I don't think I would have believed a word that came from his lips anyway. I've been sliced off into different versions of me for a year and a half now, and that slice, the slice that looks at him and knows he took you, will never give him any more. He has taken enough from this family.

So, I'm a wife, and a mum, but I'm a campaigner now too, Sarah – I fight for things. Well, I fight for children and I fight for justice. I'm fighting for you really, princess. When I go shopping, sometimes people hug me and they cry. How odd is that? You still touch them, and they feel that they can offload all of their grief about you onto me; as if there is another slice of me that *isn't* your mother, I'm just someone they can talk to about how it affected them. You know that I'm not a touchy-feely person with anyone outside the family, not really, and I find their grief strange in many ways. I want to tell them they're lucky – my tears are stuck, sometimes they won't come out, and yet they're managing to weep over a stranger while I'm dry-eyed about my child. At least I am in public. I've promised myself that I will never give that to anyone, I'll never give them that slice of me. I haven't grieved in front of anyone and I don't think I ever will.

I fill my days the best I can and most of that is with the newspaper campaign. The people at the *News of the World* have been incredible: they have supported me and I genuinely feel that they are behind what I'm trying to achieve for the best of reasons. I couldn't do it without them – but, as someone said, they need me too, they need me to be the face of this, and if that's what it takes, then I'll do it. I try to involve your dad all the time, Sarah. I always seek his agreement and I always tell him what's happening, but he doesn't really want any part of it. He'll stand beside me when he has to, but he's sinking so far into the loss of you that I don't know if he'll ever find his way out. I think I'm finding that I can use my past life to get through parts of this one, but Dad can't do that. It's about me slicing myself up again. When I was Sara the barmaid I could read people and I could talk to anyone; those elements of the old me have been far more useful than I could ever have imagined at the start. People seem to open up to me and I have made some lovely relationships from all of this; I can see in the hearts of many of the media people that they have gone through all of this too – they were there while we looked for you and when we found you; it has affected their lives as well. A lot of their feelings about child abuse are coming out and we all have a reason to work on this together. They're not the monsters people say they are; they aren't unfeeling. Most of them have been so kind to me from the very start. Your dad doesn't seem to see that; he thinks that they're a completely different breed and that this is just a job to them. But I disagree – I really believe this can make a difference.

The figures are shocking and I don't think the general public truly knows how big a problem this is. We all know it happens, we all know children are abused, but this many? It's an absolute plague, Sarah, it really is – and all the while we protect the abusers rather than the abused. I want to empower children to talk, and I want us to hear their voices so that this can be stopped. We can all make a difference – you, me, and these journalists I can now call my friends. I think, like everyone else, I have buried my head in the sand about this issue – I thought someone else would deal with it and I never wanted it to come anywhere near my little family. But my little family will never be the same again because some man, somewhere, has decided that what he wants is more important than your life. That happens far too often. Actually, if it happens once, it is far too often.

I think we have the attention of the nation after what has happened to you, darling, and I think we need to act quickly – people know. There is a need for change and it needs to be done right. When I was a barmaid, I could always sense when someone was going to be ready for a fight – I didn't need to wait until the end of the night, I knew as soon as someone like that walked through the door. I can sense a fight brewing here, but this time, I'm going to be right at the centre of it. I know I'll never be able to go back to my old life. I'll never even be able to work at a normal job again because I'll always be recognised as your mum. That's fine — I *will* always be your mum, but I need to accept that change and do what I can with it.

This campaign I've started — it's what's needed and I think it will all be sorted pretty quickly. The people of this country are good people, they know what should be happening and they are behind us, Sarah. It's common sense. Once it's done, then I'll stop, then I'll think, but for now, I have to keep moving. I'm getting bags full of mail. When we first lost you, people wrote from all over the world about the little girl who had touched their hearts. I would get envelopes that simply said, '*Sarah's Mum*', and they'd find me. Now, I still get some of those letters but I get many more, and they're all in support, they're all saying it's time to stop keeping secrets. It's time to support children when they tell, and stop looking after the paedophiles. We keep their secrets far too carefully. How can anyone say that's right? How can anyone say that's a mindset that doesn't need changing?

There are so many sad stories from elderly people who have kept their abuse secret for decades. It ruins lives. Even when people 'move on', even when they grow up, have families, think it's in the past, it comes back — or maybe it's always there. I get letters from people who still regret never telling, and I get letters from those who did tell and were never believed.

Sometimes I wish they'd talk to someone else.

How awful is that of me? I know that many, many people are hurting, but I'm hurting too. I'm carrying so much, Sarah, and I feel that, because I seem so strong, I keep getting given more. I'm trying to embed it all in the work I'm doing, but there is such a fight to put on a face. Even when people say they know it must be hard, they know I must be grieving (won't I be grieving forever?), they give me more to carry. Maybe that's my fault, maybe I should say something. How funny is that, though? We're back to secrets. We're back to not really telling the truth about what's happening. Am I as guilty of that as everyone else? Perhaps.

I feel as if the people who write to me and tell me about their abuse are giving it all to me so that I can do something with it, and I also wonder how long I have. Will the public stop supporting me? Will they get fed up of me always putting this horrible truth in front of them? I don't think so, I don't think they are like that, but there are days when I wonder how I can possibly feel I know anything. The grief becomes so big and the strength it takes to go on is so draining, I wonder whether I have any hold on anything. I don't tell other people's secrets, but I do give them a voice. Am I silencing myself while I do that? I'm helping them put their ghosts to rest, but it comes with a price. The price is you, Sarah: you allowed it. They can only reveal these things to me because I am the woman who lost her daughter to a monster.

And yet these people are the very ones who I feel can carry me through. They are the ones who I think can change things and help me make sure that Sarah's Law is something that becomes entrenched forever. But there are some who disagree, my darling — there are politicians and there are commentators and there are journalists on the other side who say there will be riots, they say people will use the information they are given and go mad with it. I feel so very, very strongly about this, princess — it just won't happen. People *won't* riot, they just won't. It's not the British way. If anyone does get it wrong, it will be because that is their mindset anyway — people like that will always be looking for an excuse to be violent or cause trouble. They are looking for an outlet, looking for a fight. Sarah's Law would be an excuse for people like that. I guess that's the barmaid in me talking! It's not about the last pint, it never is — it's about how they feel before they even step foot in the pub, and I won't have your memory being used as an excuse for people like that, my love. Politicians need to be the barmaids now — they need to read the crowd.

I've had a lot of letters, not just from the 'man on the street', but from prisoners too. The truth is, I don't want that, I don't want to bring any of that into your world. I do believe there's a difference between someone making a silly mistake or someone who makes a calculated choice that ruins life, but sometimes I just want to close everything off, Sarah — I just want to think about you and what I can do in your memory in a little bubble. Is that so wrong of me? Maybe not when you know some of the other things I've been subjected to. Anything I do is filtered through this, I know that, but one journalist has said I've been blindsided by fame, that I'm loving all of this, and that it was my fault as I should never have let you play alone. Always the woman's fault, isn't it, darling? Your dad let you play with Lee and Luke and Charlotte too, but he's not subjected to this sort of horrible comment. People like her – that journalist – does she really look at me and think I'm in my element? Does she think I want this? All I want is you. I would have happily lived my life out in peace, with all my children, *all* my children. I would have been delighted to never know of the media, never to be on the speed dial of them all, never to have seen my face on television screens and front pages.

It's disgusting.

It's disgusting that another human being – I'll say it, another *woman* – can think that way, never mind repeat it for millions to read. Is that what some are thinking of me, though? Is she just saying what others are saying behind my back? I hear from people who support me, and I hear from broken people, I hear from prisoners and I hear from parents; but what about the ones I don't hear from? What are they saying? What do their whispers say about me? That it's my fault, that I deserve this; I'm glorying in it? It hurts, Sarah, it hurts. But it doesn't hurt as much as being without you, so I will rise above it. I will blank these people if they say these things in a newspaper column with their picture and their name proudly displayed to the world, and I will try not to think about the ones who hide in their shallow little worlds. And I will even hope that none of this ever touches them, because I wouldn't wish it on my worst enemy.

This year has been so hard, princess, hard in many ways. There was once a little boy who went missing, just like you. This little boy – James Bulger – was found much more quickly than you were, but his ending was just as dark. James had been taken away by two boys, two *children*, who did terrible things to him, and who finally killed that poor angel. He wasn't even three years old when he died; he was never even given a chance to live, taken from his mother in a shopping centre, in broad daylight – taken, just as you were, by strangers who should never even have crossed paths with him.

And now, those strangers, those two boys – now young men – are to be released and given new identities so that they can lead a life free from people knowing who they are and what they did. This is their right, we are all told. These lives they are to be granted are what they are entitled to after they committed the most horrific acts anyone could imagine.

This protection makes me want to scream. Every time I hear of a perpetrator being given protection, being given an opportunity to experience what they denied their victim, I feel as if Sarah's Law is slipping away. I know Denise, James's mum, and I know their story well. I knew it before you were taken – everyone in the country did. We all followed the stories on the news with the grainy images which showed the two boys taking the toddler by the hand and leading him away, while Denise was distracted for just a second. We all saw later images where they walked down streets with him, walked towards the railway line where he would be tortured and abused, watched the horror of a child trustingly walking to his own death. Those images were ingrained in my mind – you were eighteen months younger than Denise's baby, and he was about the same age as our Luke when he was taken. I had watched that story unfold as a mum, never for one second imagining I would one day be in Denise's shoes.

But I am. I'm walking that path, and everything I know she is dealing with, I know is waiting for me too. When I hear about James's killers being guaranteed their freedom and the protection they 'need', I think *that's my future*.

These stories are always in the news. There always seems to be some high-profile offender who is being released or who is appealing against their conviction and all too often the child in the story is glossed over – their pain, their suffering, the loss of them. The focus is on the wrong person.

Every time a criminal is released, someone who has done awful things to a child, I'm reminded of my own mortality, Sarah. I feel as if the clock is ticking. It's always ticking, and I feel I need to change something; change the world in some way to acknowledge you were here.

I know that Whiting will always have a say in our lives – he can always appeal, I know that – and I'm terrified that the tiniest thing could bring it all down. The wall I have built is not as strong as it looks to others. The entire justice system is built for offenders, it seems. People would think of me the way they think of Denise. But I want to be something else. I want people to look at me and think of what I have achieved, what I have done for children in your name. I think it's harder for Denise – with you, my love, it was stranger danger. We're all of us, all of us parents, terrified of that, but it is rare. With James, it was other children. For Denise every day is a reminder, everything must be terrifying. Even the sound of kids playing in the street can't be one of innocence, because it was children just like those who took her child away. I had my answers quite quickly – for her, how can she ever know peace?

We've been 'awarded' £11,000 by the Criminal Injuries Compensation Board – isn't that a funny thing to call it – an 'award'? We've been given money for losing you, and it's an 'award'. I know that it doesn't matter, what it's called, but it also doesn't matter how much it is. It could be a pound or it could be a million, nothing can compensate, but it's started a huge debate on the value of a child's life. The £11,000 was the most we could have been given, because a child's life is valued in a different way. You weren't an adult when you were taken from us, so we're not struggling without your earnings, without your weekly wage – that's what I was told. You didn't bring money into the family, so we don't feel the lack of that.

I need to distance myself from this sort of talk or I'll go mad.

How much were you worth, princess, how much were you worth?

I was never interested in the money. I was influenced into filling in the forms by the advice of the police and others – they said we were entitled, that it was the least that could be done for us. It's true that Dad can't work any more. He just hasn't been able to step back into that world, and we did need the money, but I do feel you've been . . . I guess the word would be 'diminished'. I feel you've been diminished by a value being put on your life, darling. Now that the money has come through, it's been a double slap. Millions wouldn't have been enough, there's nothing that would compensate. This is the system's way of saying 'sorry' though; they're not really compensating, they're just acknowledging it has happened, which is fair enough. People seem to feel it's fair game for them to ask me what we'll spend it on, as if we've had a windfall, as if we've won the lottery.

But I think you know what I've spent a lot of it on, don't you, Sarah? I think you've seen the angel, the beautiful stone angel that stands over your grave now, watching you as you sleep, watching you when I can't be there.

Do you see everything? Were you there in November 2001 at the end of the year when we went to court? This is something else that I'm torn about – do I want to talk to you about him? No, not really – but it's part of your story, isn't it? It's part of it all. I had built it up so much, Sarah. All along, I knew I'd be there at the first court appearance, at the plea hearing.

And, do you know what it was?

It was nothing.

He was so cold. He turned up, pleaded 'Not Guilty' ('Not Guilty' – he didn't even have the decency to admit what he'd done), then he was taken back to prison.

That was it.

I'd built him up as this great big monster and it turned out he was so insignificant. He wasn't even wearing a suit; he had no gravitas whatsoever. He wasn't even worried enough to brush his hair. Pathetic.

The pre-hearing lasted minutes – less time than I'd spent being violently sick beforehand, in all honesty. I'd made it into such a big deal, but it was all done and dusted with about as much emotion as a parking fine. It was nothing like the TV dramas, you see, nothing like a film. Real life is much smaller than that. The actions affect more people and they last for longer, but the actors, the sets . . . they're little things.

By the time of the trial, I suppose I'd thought it would be a confrontation but it was quick and dismissive. The families of the victim aren't really allowed to be a part of it. The family liaison officers never left our sides, and we had your dad's brother as well as my mum and dad with us, but the harsh truth is, it's just a procedure: we were visitors. The police were quite calm about everything and I guess they hoped that would rub off on us, but they had to be – they were on show. I kept being told this was the biggest case the country had ever seen and I couldn't quite relate that to my little girl. How had it come to this? How had our lives come to this? There had been talk of having the session in Sussex, but Whiting's team said he wouldn't get a fair trial there. A fair trial! When had he been fair to you? Why did it always come down to treating the killers and the abusers well? He was nothing to be feared or revered. It was such a small room and I was sat right next to the dock. He didn't look at me once, but I couldn't take my eyes off him.

Dirty.

Scruffy.

Detestable.

So, why had I allowed him so much power? It was a turning point for me, really. I can't give him anything more; I *won't* give him anything more. Why have I been allowing him to ruin what is left of my children's lives?

I made a vow in that courtroom, Sarah – and I hope you heard it. That vow was to him: she thinks – *you're having no more of me.*

I have obsessed, I'll admit it, but I can see the truth now: you were just in the wrong place at the wrong time, my darling. I needed perspective and, oddly, Whiting is the one who has given it to me. It's not the same for your dad — he wanted Whiting to be more. He's too 'nothing'. I think Dad looked at him and thought *I could take him; I could take him in a fight, he's so pathetic* and it made him feel useless. It made him feel even worse.

I was terrified — about the boys, about Charlotte, about the case ... about absolutely everything. Every day, we were smuggled in through the back door as if we were the villains. Sometimes Charlotte and the boys came, but I know people didn't approve of that. I fought for them to be there on the last day but I didn't want them near him, especially Lee, given that he had seen him when you were taken. I internalise a lot, an awful lot. I think Nanny sees it, perhaps not as much as there really is, but she's been staying with us for a while, and she can't miss it — she has that mother's instinct too. She's lost her granddaughter as well, and I need to recognise that, but I have so many people to look after, Sarah — and I'm so very tired. Nanny does hug me, she does give me a cuddle, but her view is that this is the hand I've been dealt, so I just need to get on with it. She's very matter-of-fact, even though her heart is broken too — or maybe she's just like that when she's trying to help me through. It's the only way she knows, I guess.

When I saw him, I felt so physically sick. I was shaking, my memory gave up; I was in shock, really but I didn't realise it. Every day when the FLOs picked us up and took us to court, I would think *maybe I'll be OK today.* How could I be, though? How could I be?

I think I had my biggest wobble when the jury went out at the end. There was a part of me that thought *what if he gets away with it?* I'm not stupid, I've seen it happen – it just takes one mistake in the line of evidence, one word out of place, and someone like him is laughing his way to freedom. I knew it had been proven forensically, but I needed to be there to make sure justice would be served. I thought the jury would be back in a few minutes, I really did, but when they didn't come back that day, or the next, I started to wobble again.

I started to worry needlessly that the whole thing would have to be done again. The case was of such interest that the jury became of interest. They would occasionally look at me – when he was on the stand they looked at me; I soon realised that. Maybe they wanted to see how I would react or maybe they just didn't want to look at him, who knows?

I never took my eyes off him, but he didn't seem bothered. He didn't cast so much as a glance at us. I wanted him to show regret, but it soon became clear that he wasn't that sort of person. He had been 'out on the prowl', he said, and that dismissive phrase just showed to me that you were just unlucky, sweetheart, just unlucky. You could have been anyone, any little girl. When people say, 'Don't you wonder why you've had to go through this?', I always think, 'Why not?' and it's true. Why not us? Why not me? Why not you? We're not special; we're not better than any other family, so why shouldn't we be the ones to face this?

Had he admitted it at the beginning, he would have saved us all those months of pain, but he wouldn't even do that. I knew it was him from very early on because the police told us everything but the jury didn't know his past history – they weren't allowed to know what sort of man he was. That is wrong. I felt it then, I feel it now, and I will always feel it: juries need to know what someone is capable of. After it was over, after he was found guilty, one of the jurors was in tears when the list of past crimes was read out. Not only did he waste time, and take energy, and prolong our grief, but he even took resources away from those who need them. If millions hadn't been poured into his sham of a defence, then perhaps they could have gone elsewhere, somewhere that could have helped children, somewhere that would have protected those who need to be protected, rather than indulge the guilty.

I wanted the kids to hear that word, to hear GUILTY, just the boys – it was part of their lives. They were just inside the door with my dad, with grandad; I couldn't see them or get to them, and that was painful, but if I went to them, it would alert everyone that they were there.

Sometimes his mum was there.

Sometimes his sister.

They were watching – but he never looked at them either.

And I would think, *we're going through hell, but so are they. We have each other – look at what they have to deal with.*

I felt deeply for his mother, as a mum myself. I genuinely

didn't feel she was responsible because I think everyone needs to take control of what they have done, of their own actions. He chose to be what he was; he chose to do what he did. His mother didn't do that for him, so I didn't blame her for any of it. At one point, his mum and my mum were next to each other – there was a barrier between them, but nothing else. I don't think either of them was aware of it, but I was; by God, I was. They were both in so much pain.

I made a public statement afterwards – were you listening? I couldn't read the police one, the words were flying about, and so I spoke from the heart, as always. I suppose the main thing I felt was that we had justice, but it changed nothing.

I went home dead, stunned.

Nothing had changed, nothing had changed.

You still weren't with us.

It *should* have changed something.

Twelve people had said it was true, twelve people had said he was to blame, but I knew that already – so what was I expecting to change?

I think I'm getting harder now, Sarah – I think I'll need to be. In the weeks that have been since he was found guilty, it's been all about him, his story, his reasons, his excuses … But what about you? I don't care about him; I care about you.

Whiting will be released one day, I know it: one day, who knows when, he will convince someone he feels remorse, he will tell his side of things, he will make up lies, he will remind people he has rights – and he will be freed. He may be an old man by then, but he has taken your right to ever be an old woman. He took your right to everything, but that won't be enough for him – he will want to be free as well.

I'm looking back on this year, Sarah, and I can't believe how much there's been. There have been huge events like a terrorist attack in America that made people say the world has changed forever, but mine changed in the summer of 2000. Often I think it's the little things that hit the hardest. I read all of the 'Harry Potter' books to keep me distracted this year and to keep me in touch with anything to do with magic, because you loved it so, but when I watched the film come out, that affected me a lot. You were such a magical child and you would have adored it. You believed in fairies and the softer side of childhood, and you would have been pestering me with tales of Hogwarts from the day the film was launched, wouldn't you? People might find that sad, but I gave you what I could for the short time you were with me. Now that you're not here, the stories and the magic go on – you're just watching them from somewhere else.

I hope your 'somewhere else' is beautiful, my darling, I hope you're at peace there. xx

2002

DEAR SARAH —

Life goes on, this year, every year, and the most wonderful thing of all is there is happiness, there are smiles. We moved house this year, darling — hard, because we left some good memories behind, but necessary, because of the bad ones. It was odd to think we were going on without you, but I've known since the start that the world keeps turning — I just have to find my peace with that. I was so angry that the world wasn't affected, that things didn't shut down, at the beginning, but now I have to accept that even the people who loved you most move on. Some people said to me, 'It'll become old news'. By *it*, they meant you, of course; even the police said that the journalists would get fed up and leave. But they didn't. In some ways no one has forgotten — the journalists may not be outside the house any more, but they're still calling me, sometimes just to see how I am. So, the world has changed, but it also hasn't changed at all.

I still have the wall around me, princess — I think I always will. I had such awful nightmares when you went missing, and I thought they would get better over time, but they've been much, much worse this year. So dark, so awful, but not really about anything detailed. I wake up feeling so fearful, Sarah, but then I remember my worst nightmare already came true. There doesn't seem to be any colour in my dreams and I never have any nice ones about you. Sometimes, I would do anything for just a few minutes in my sleep, seeing you again, holding you again. I never seem to get those. It makes me terrified of going to bed, so I'm staying up later and later. I've been like that since you left, and I'd watch almost anything, preferring comedy if I could find it, but, recently, I've started watching crime drama — any crime drama, no matter how horrible, no matter how close to home. I devour it, always desperate for things to turn out well, or for the perpetrator to get caught. It's not like watching my life, not the real one. It's a version I can accept, a different version of my reality. I look forward to the end of the episode or the series or the film; I look forward to all the ends being tied up, knowing *my* loose ends will never be so neatly sorted.

I still buy too many groceries; I still cook for one more. I still set a place at the table for you. Do you remember that you used to have tomato sauce with everything? Especially eggs and chips! You would have so much sauce on top of it that you could hardly see the food. Now, there are too many bottles of unused ketchup in the kitchen cupboard. No one says anything, it's just ignored, but I want you to know that I haven't forgotten, that I still remember your favourite things and I want to take care of you forever. I can see a sadness in Lee and Luke and Charlotte – maybe they don't ignore it as well as I think they do. I need to pull myself together, don't I? They have such long lives ahead of them, such futures, and I don't want everything to be defined by this.

I can see now that it has hit Charlotte the worst. She's the only sister, not the little one. That has been such an adjustment and she's been affected the most in so many ways. Lee and Luke's friendship groups haven't really changed. I'm not saying it's been easy for them, far from it, but they still have each other. With Charlotte – well, she has a bedroom to herself now and she hates it. I know she sneaks into the boys' room and they let her stay, but it's not what she had with you, Sarah. I still have all of your things, darling (I'm keeping them until I feel able to cope with getting rid of them one day, but I doubt that day will ever come), and Charlotte will sometimes take a dress, or a jumper, and she'll just keep it close to her.

I still have so many of the teddies and soft toys that were left for you too. There were dozens of bin bags filled with what was left at the side of the road for you and although we gave hundreds away, to charities, I've brought far too many of them here. I know that's silly because you never saw them, you never touched them, so they aren't really part of you. I also know that it's the charity side of it you would have loved. One group boxed up so many of them to be sent to Kosovo for kids who have nothing in the midst of the horror there, and you would have wanted that to happen.

These months have been so long – and you've stayed eight years old throughout. I guess you always will. I'm not the only one who's struggling – a lot of your little friends from school are too. So many of you had been together since you were three, since you were no more than toddlers at nursery, and I know they've also had horror brought into their young lives. I don't know how their parents have dealt with it, though; I guess they all have different ways to explain what happened to Sarah Payne. When I see them, perhaps at the shops, perhaps walking along the street, I feel so angry – not at them, but at the world. It's such a stark reminder when I see them growing, laughing, living … You'll never do any of that.

Part of me despises other people's happiness. I get jealous – isn't that awful? Then I have a word with myself. I shouldn't begrudge anyone happiness, not for a second. I wish I had something to cling to. I'm not religious but sometimes I think that would be a nice, easy option – I could just let everything float. Now I know in my heart it causes more problems than it solves and if there were a God there wouldn't be more families who continued to be put through this horror. But this year, yet again, another Mum and Dad are dealing with it all; another family is facing the horrors we faced. A young girl called Milly Dowler went missing, and, because she lived just down the road from where we used to be, the press all turned to me again. As soon as it happened, as soon as it hit the headlines, I felt again as if there were more bad people than good in the world. It doesn't seem so long since it was our family going through this; I was the mum they haunted, the one whose face was on every news bulletin. I couldn't sleep with it all, when the news about Milly broke – but I haven't slept since the summer you went. This year, I just had something else to focus on. I found myself speaking at 3am to journalists working on the story; when I was asked to write an article to Milly's abductor, it took me back to 2000.

I feel strongly about this – why would the family of someone who is missing want me involved? After all, I represent the worst possible outcome. If there's any hope at all, you don't want to see me. I was sure that Milly's family wanted their own voice, just as they wanted their own child, but I will always help where I can. I'll talk if I'm asked, I'll give a comment if it will help, I'll say what it's like being part of the circus that springs up, but I'll only do so if it's wanted. People often ask what to me was the biggest shock about everything that happened, Sarah, but the biggest shock of all was that it happened in the first place. Once I was part of it all, once *we* were part of it all, the media became friends, as you know, and I can't regret that they were there because of what's been achieved with their help since then. But they do own you. They own pretty much all of me, but that's a price I'll pay. People who think that I enjoy the celebrity side just a little too much, would they pay this price? As far as I'm concerned it's a life in the public eye without any of the good bits.

I'm still getting so much in the way of response from the public. I do appreciate what most of them are trying to do, but I hate it when they talk about bringing hanging back or what they would do to 'him'. It's offensive to you. You're eight, my darling, you're still only eight — you shouldn't have to hear these things, you shouldn't be associated with them. Every discussion I have seems to be about paedophilia — people think they know what to do; they have all the answers. They still say they would die if this happened to them, and they also say they would kill the person who did it. I haven't done either of those things — does that make me a bad mother?

I know I'm still in shock; I know that. It won't ever go, but I feel so protective of the others. If they're with me when people start ranting, then I push them behind me, I want to keep them from the horrible things that are being said, despite the fact that they have been in the middle of it since that summer. I don't want strangers talking to them; I don't want strangers trying to get a piece of them. I always try to keep Charlotte close, to put her on my hip and turn her face away; I do wonder how much they hear though, how much they take in. Charlotte seems so bewildered at times but I'm stumbling through the days and I wonder whether I'm doing everything I need to for her. She sometimes still asks why she has to sleep alone and that makes everything so raw. I remember the way you used to be tangled up in each other, you'd never push her away if she came into your bed. You were so kind, so gentle – and she doesn't have that now. She has lost her big sister and sometimes I feel that she's lost her mother too.

And your brothers? I don't think they have much trust in the world anyway. Something's gone forever with them. They're consumed by guilt, I can see that – especially Lee. He feels so responsible and I wonder if he'll ever move past it. I know he thinks it was his fault – and I know there are people who tell them it was. Neither of them want long-term counselling; they don't trust anyone enough to stick with it. They did have a few sessions at the start, but their lack of trust made sure it would never work. They don't think anyone outside of the family is on their side. . . no one was to be trusted.

They don't go for counselling any more. I think the fact that we weren't allowed to speak about it all before the trial was a bad thing. It meant that we developed a habit of *not* speaking about it at all. If we had been allowed to be open then, to have the tears, to have a family that could speak about everything, that would have changed how we are now. But the evidence had to be preserved, their words had to be kept from any influence. How ridiculous is that? We all knew what had happened, there was nothing that needed to be made up because the reality was bad enough. The only outcome from those months and months was that Lee and Luke kept it all in; they were just little boys who were being asked to behave like adults, with something happening in their lives that few adults could deal with.

When we visit Nanny and Grandad, we pass the field, darling. We pass *that* field. I know that I always say life goes on, but I swear, in those moments, it almost stops. I can feel the sadness of the place. It's as if something of you has been left there, that your memory and your soul have left an imprint that reaches out every time we walk past. I want to go there, but I hate it too. Lee and Luke and Charlotte feel it too, but, we never speak about it. It makes me wonder whether we've tried to be too normal. Afterwards, it was back to school, back to life, back to day-to-day, but was that the right way? I have no idea.

Just when I thought I could breathe again, another two little girls disappeared this year, two ten-year-old friends called Holly Wells and Jessica Chapman. It's been another summer of screaming headlines, day after day of lies and hope, of interviews and press conferences, and then, at the end of it, another man who was known, another man who should have been stopped long ago.

Holly and Jessica have touched everyone's hearts just as you did; and their parents have faced the same horrors, with many of the same kindnesses and the same cruelties. One journalist even said their parents were to blame because if they had observed the Sabbath and kept them inside rather than allowing them out to play, they would never have been taken. I'm always stunned by the way people can be so kind, but so cruel too. The cruelty of those words, the cruelty of feeling that you should put thoughts like that out there, beggars belief – I don't know how people like that can sleep at night.

I think the murders of Holly and Jessica hit everyone hard. It was so frightening to many people because the two of them were together, they should have been safe. With you, people always had some sort of hope in a strange sort of way – stranger danger, being taken by someone who isn't known to the child . . . it's all so unusual. The danger usually comes from within families or from people the child trusts; that didn't happen with you, so there were always the statistics to comfort people. It was heartbreaking, but it was also incredibly rare. With Holly and Jessica, they were together, they were close to home, they were happy and loved – and yet, they were still in danger. When it came out that, again, that it was someone they knew, that their school caretaker Ian Huntley had broken their trust and his girlfriend Maxine Carr had tried to protect him, the nation was in shock again. There has been a lot of blaming of Carr, even more so than Huntley, because it's hard for people to accept that a woman can be involved in anything like this. They think, they hope, that there is still some sort of caring side to all women that will make children safe if they are involved, but that's just the sort of deluded thinking I'm trying to tackle with Sarah's Law – it's the children who matter, not anyone else's notion of what is safe and what isn't.

Everyone was in shock about those little girls. It was too soon: the country hadn't recovered from you, yet here we were back to square one. The journalists who worked the case were the ones who had covered you, the ones I knew and who were now friends. I've ended up counselling so many of them. You, Milly, James, Holly, Jessica … it's a lot of darkness to deal with in so little time. They all know I can't sleep, so they call me at all hours, in the middle of the night when their minds are racing, or when they're waiting on the next development. And I tried to recognise their pain; I didn't resent them at all or see it as an intrusion. In fact, sometimes it was comforting to speak to them, to know there was someone else out there feeling it in the same way. All I really felt was disgust for Huntley and for what he had done to those families. I knew what was coming next for them, just how bad it would be.

I've always believed in life after death, you know that, and I hope with every part of me that my words to you this summer have reached you, darling. Do you remember? Do you remember what I said when they were found? *I need you to do something for me now: keep Holly and Jessica safe, princess. When they get there, meet them, show them how things are done where you are; show them the way. You're a good girl,*

you won't leave them alone. They'll be so scared to start with, but
you'll look after them, I know that. You can do more than I can.

Did you do that, Sarah? Did you look out for them and
take care of them? I hope you're all together, safe and
happy.

I can see you smiling, but I wish you could answer
me back, sweetheart. You were such a caring girl – you
are such a caring girl – and you were always the first
to look after a lost or lonely child. Do you remember
the befriender bench they had at school? I swear you
were there every day, just checking, just looking to see
if anyone needed you. You were doing all of those kind
things long before anyone had thought of a bench. Such
a mother hen ... I know you would have always been
that way and it comforts me to think that you still have
that nature. Your heart was so big, Sarah, and I hope you
can still help, that you can still look after any lost souls
who come your way.

Why do people always care more about the monsters?
Myra Hindley died a few weeks ago and all I could think
was, *thank God, they'll never let her out now* because I truly
feared that would have been the case, and she would have
been given protection. It had gone on so long that people
were forgetting – they were making excuses for her and
thinking it was in the past. Not for the parents it wasn't,
not for those families. I do believe that a person can change
but there shouldn't be the opportunity to forget what they
have done. No chances should be taken where children are

concerned: they're not guinea pigs and the people who do these things know exactly what they're doing at the time.

Christmas hasn't been great again this year – I really haven't made much of an effort, and I feel bad about that. I'm a mum of four, not a mum of one. The kids aren't really interested in Christmas, but they need to be – they still need to love it all. I think they, we, are deadened to happiness, princess – but who knows? Maybe this time next year we will have moved on, at least a little. I need to try and make sure they don't see this as a competition. You'll always be eight, whereas they will get older, our relationships will be harder. When you're a stroppy teenager, you can't compete with the memory of a dead eight-year-old, and that's the harsh truth.

You will always be soft and good. You will always be the angel that you have been painted as, and that's fine, because you were like that. However, I have other angels, and they matter too.

Do you know something, Sarah? I always felt you were too good for this earth; I always felt I would have to give you up early. The most awful thing is this – now that I have seen how survivors of abuse, of terrible things, are treated as adults, I don't think I would have wanted that for you. If you had come back to us after all those days away, what would you have been? You would have been ripped apart by society and by the whole process survivors go through. For you there would have been no support, you would have been left to pick up the pieces and people would forget. The press, the social services, the whole country … how much would they have loved you ten, twenty years down the line when you were still broken? And how would you have coped with life when you were always 'that' Sarah Payne? Anything you did for the rest of your life would have been blamed on it, and you would never have been allowed an ordinary life. Every anniversary, every time something happened in your world, you would be tracked down. I know that every time a child goes missing, I'm contacted. Every time there is the possibility that another little one has been taken, they come to me. That would never have stopped – maybe I would have represented hope in a way that I don't these days, but maybe I would have just represented the mother of the girl who was broken forever. I don't know what either of us would have become, darling, but I can't imagine it would have been a fairytale. How could such a gentle soul as you have dealt with all of that? How would you have got past what had been done to you by him? Once life gives you a hardness, you can't return to your innocence.

I would do anything to step back in time and not have it happen, but once it did?

No.

I've seen what the court process does to victims and it's vile. I wouldn't put you through that, my darling.

I keep thinking that, if you had been found, you would have forgiven him. That's painful, because I'm not as good as you: I can't forgive or forget.

I've learned that I can cope and I can survive. I get so cross when people say to me, 'Oh, I could never get through something like this – I'd never be able to', or, 'It would crush me, I would die myself if anything happened to my child'. How dare they! How dare they presume to know how I feel, and how dare they presume to suggest that they are more emotional than me, that I'm colder because I'm still standing. Some days, I don't know how I even get up in the morning. I'm physically tired, so, so tired, unnaturally tired, all of the time, Sarah. My body *does* want to give up, but how can I let that happen? That would be such an insult to you. I just miss you so much, it's as simple and as complicated as that. It might look as if everything's OK with me, but it's really not.

I never want you to look through a window and think I've forgotten. Things are dark just now, but I always hope for the light. I just want to hear you laugh again. I think I'm almost used to the pain now; I'm so used to feeling sad that I don't think I'll ever be without it. Maybe it would be easier for people if I did give up, maybe they could relate to that. But I won't. I'll keep getting out of bed every day, I'll keep fighting. You deserve that.

You deserve to have a legacy – and I'll be that legacy for you, princess. xx

2003

DEAR SARAH —

I sometimes feel I'm just watching everything on a loop. The Criminal Injuries Compensation Board has given £11k each to the families of Holly Wells and Jessica Chapman, just like they did to us, and the same arguments are rehashed.

I'm still trying to look at it coldly. It's processed in such a way because the person being 'valued' hasn't lived, they're 'just' a child; they haven't worked or paid tax, they don't have dependants. It's just a calculation, it isn't personal — you get three times more for losing an eye than losing a child. But it has affected our lives, every part of our lives, just as it will affect theirs. I can't go back to before — 'before' doesn't exist any more. How can I work now?

I'm a public figure – how can I be a barmaid again, who would employ me? Can you imagine what it would be like to be in that sort of job? Pulling someone's pint then they clock who I am, or who they think I am. People often say to me, 'You look like that Sara Payne woman'. I just reply, 'I get that a lot.' But I do eventually admit it to some people; I'm not ashamed of who I am, but I don't want to have that conversation every time. It would be never-ending, and I can't imagine any employer taking all of my baggage on board. So, while I know that the compensation for children takes into account that they were 'just' kids, the loss of them so often means that no one can ever go back to a normal life. 'Normal' changes into something else, and my normal has changed beyond all recognition.

Dad and I have fallen apart so much, darling, and things have been so sad. Your Uncle Paul passed away this year: he died of cancer and I was heartbroken. I couldn't believe that my big, strong brother had also gone forever, that I'd lost someone else, but sometimes things work in mysterious ways. Your dad and I have hardly ever been close and he's rarely here, but there was one night when we both had far too much to drink and ended up closer than we had been since you left. We're still married to each other, and it was a fling within our relationship really, and we knew that we are in the middle of something very toxic when we are together, but somehow, somehow . . .

How do I explain this, darling?

How do I explain it to an eight-year-old?

Truthfully, I guess.

Sarah, you're going to be a big sister again!

I need your help, princess. I need you to do something for me. You're going to be a big sister again as it's through some sort of miracle that I'm having another baby. Your dad and I have somehow managed to make something wonderful and precious from the toxic mess of our dead relationship, and I need that baby to be safe. Will you help me?

I think this baby was meant to be. Our anger and our fights had been forgotten for that one night, that one moment, and this baby is the result. Do I want to bring another child into the world? I'll struggle with it, that's for sure. I had four children and one had been taken from me, but I can't bring myself to say I have one less. I think it's something every grieving parent has to address. When people ask you how many children you have, it's the hardest question in the world. I gave birth to four, I am the mother of four — do I not count you because you're not here? Do I get bogged down in saying that I *had* four, but now I *have* three? No, I'll never dismiss you in that way. If people get confused, they can just ask questions. If they ask your ages, I will tell them about my eight-year-old who will stay eight forever. I'll never erase you from my life, or from our family history just because it's easier for anyone else. If they ask the question, they have to be able to deal with the answer and all the baggage that comes with it.

There will be nine years between this new baby and Charlotte – and I think that the biggest shock will be that Charlotte has moved from little sister to only girl, and she will now take your place as the big sister. I'm not sure that she's ready for that, but I'll do all I can to help her. Actually, she'll still have you in my mind – the new baby will have two big sisters, but how much will that register with little Charlotte? How much should I say about that? I always answer her questions, but she sometimes goes into herself and doesn't ask me things. I will tell her that you are looking out for the new baby too, but she's still so little herself that I don't want to burden her. I just really hope that she gets some happiness from the arrival of this little one; I hope we all do.

I'm not sure that I can write as much as I've been writing, darling – I'm not sure it's good for me or for you. The last two Christmases, when I've sat down and thought of all that has happened, I do feel that I should be looking forward, that I ought to be looking at the children I still have with me. I hope that doesn't sound as if I'm leaving you behind, princess, I'll never do that, but I need to make sure that this baby comes into a family a lot less broken than we are just now.

I know you'll be happy with my news. I know you always loved babies, and that you won't think I'm trying to replace you in any way, because that could never happen, but sometimes . . . sometimes I just need to breathe.

★

Such strange times, Sarah, such strange times.

I was giving a speech to the Police Federation Conference in May when I started to feel unwell. There were lots of journalists with me from the *News of the World*, and I was giving a talk about Sarah's Law to the biggest audience I'd ever been in front of.

I remember saying to someone, 'I feel so odd.'

'Are you nervous?' they asked me. 'It's probably just nerves.'

'I don't get nervous!' I replied, and I was telling the truth. 'I just do these things – I never really think of who I'm speaking to and I always just tell it from the heart so I don't have anything to get nervous about, but this just feels . . . odd. I don't know what it is.'

I wondered if the baby was maybe just moving about, or I'd picked up a bug somewhere. On the train home, it got much worse. I was dizzy, I felt faint – something just wasn't right. By the time I got to the station, I knew something was dreadfully wrong – and then the bleeding started.

I was rushed to hospital by ambulance, with a couple of the hacks who had been with me, and they sat and waited while everything went on. I knew they'd keep it private; I knew they were there as friends. The bleeding was so bad – I guessed there was no hope, but you just keep trying to hold it together, knowing that whatever is thrown at you, you'll have to deal with it, no matter what.

'I've lost the baby, haven't I?' I said to the ambulance

driver as I was wheeled out. 'There can't be all of this pain unless something has gone very wrong.'

'We'll just have to wait and see, love,' he replied, patting me on the hand. 'Let's leave it to the experts.'

But I knew.

I think he did too.

I was taken to the scanning room with a nurse chattering away, trying to be normal, while all the time I knew that my baby had died. There was absolutely no possibility that this wasn't the outcome – there had been too much blood and too much pain. It wasn't meant to be.

Everyone was kind, but as someone squirted the cold gel onto my tummy, I could hardly bear to look at the screen. There would only be bad news.

Someone squeezed my hand, someone else smiled, but these were gestures of sympathy, not encouragement.

The room was very quiet.

As it should be, I suppose, when things go wrong.

'I'm so sorry, Sara,' the sonographer said, 'the sac is empty – you've lost the baby.'

It was no surprise.

I waited for them to wipe the gel off and take me back to the ward, but it was taking a while – I assumed they needed to have lots of images, to make sure that it was all in the right order for my file. The bleeding had stopped a bit, and the pain wasn't quite so bad, but the baby had died and I just wanted to get back to the ward and then, hopefully, home as soon as possible.

'Sara . . .' someone ventured, gently.

'I'm fine – it's fine,' I answered, even though they hadn't asked.

'Good, good . . . it's just . . .'

'What?' I asked. 'Is everything OK?' I knew it wasn't but I dreaded there was something else, that something else was wrong.

It turns out, princess, there was something else – but the most wonderful thing!

'Sara – there's still a baby,' one of the nurses said.

'No – how can there be?' I replied.

'Twins,' came the answer. 'You were pregnant with twins!'

I looked at the screen and there it was.

A heartbeat.

Life. Still fighting.

A miracle from you, darling?

I was blown away by this news, and from that point on I've never doubted this pregnancy was meant to be. I did have my moments when I'd wondered whether it was the right thing, but not any longer. This little one is special and I'm so grateful to be pregnant still.

Of course, there has been a loss, but I can compart-mentalise grief. It's what I'm good at – I've had so much darkness in my life that it's water off a duck's back.

I think, as the pregnancy has gone on, I've lost a bit of the happiness I felt that night. This baby is a girl, another little girl, and that has brought a mixed bag of confusion and blessings. I'm all over the place, really. I probably would be anyway, with all of the pregnancy hormones rushing about and losing one of the babies, but I don't know whether I'm coming or going. There's no excitement, and that's a horrible feeling. A new life should be celebrated, but I'm just deadened. Losing my brother has been so hard. I've lost a sibling now too; although to cancer, not in the way Lee and Luke and Charlotte lost you, there is still something about a sibling's death that brings a different sadness to other bereavements. He was such a big, tall, strong Army man; I honestly thought nothing could touch him.

It's made me think about my own mortality too. Being pregnant at this age, at thirty-five, is very different to how it was in my twenties. I'm tired, and I'm also not the same woman. This baby is going to be a fighter – I just hope I have the strength to fight beside her.

Dad and I are trying to show the world a united front, but it's all fake – it's all to make out that we are a strong family, waiting for this new child. Do you know that 98 per cent of marriages break up after murder? Of course I never wanted to be one of those statistics, but I have to accept that I am. I wanted to be the exception but I know it's beyond fixing. No relationship counsellor in the world could give us back what we've lost. I don't think either of us met the needs of the other; I'm not sure we even knew what they were. We were both closed off, both dealing with our pain internally, and only able to talk to each other when we'd had too much to drink.

That's no way to live and it's no way to bring a baby into the world either.

Everything's the wrong way round, princess. I shouldn't be confiding in an eight-year-old. If you were still here, I'd be hiding things from you, not telling you every last detail. Sometimes I feel you're the only person I can speak to. I do have good friends but even they don't know every last detail; sometimes you're the only one that I can show myself to. I think Dad and I have been so involved in our own heads that we've stopped caring about each other. Maybe this baby should have brought us together, made us see that we could try again, but the damage is done.

No child is a mistake, and I believe that we are all on a certain road in life. For that one night, your dad and I tried to put a plaster on the wound that is our marriage, but it's all pretence. I know that people are thinking we're OK, and I also know that I'm contributing to that by putting on a front, but I can't bear for your brothers and sister to know that it's broken beyond repair.

Do you remember when I used to tell you that people would say thoughtless things about how they would never have coped if 'this' had happened to them? How they would never survive if their child was murdered? Or the ones who would tell me in great detail what they would do to paedophiles if they 'dared' touch their child? Well, they have something new to be insensitive about now. I have lost count of the numbers who have asked whether this baby will 'make up' for you, or even whether I'll call her Sarah.

As if you could be replaced!

As if any child could be replaced.

No, this little girl will be her own person. She's already a fighter, already she's had to make her mark on the world, and I'm convinced she'll be her own person. I'll never compare her to you. She'll know all about her wonderful big sister, but she'll never feel that she's second place. I'll never allow that. It will be so hard to look at an innocent child in my arms again and not be terrified, but that's what we all have to do: we have to deal with things. And won't it be wonderful if the cloud lifts for just a little while and there is something to celebrate?

Your dad and I have split up now, Sarah – but it's for the best. He moved into the dining room downstairs for a little while before announcing that he'd found a place close by. It made me go on autopilot, really – I was numb. It just happened: there wasn't one big thing, it was just years of being toxic with each other and finally seeing it doesn't have to be that way, there can be a different life. We hadn't been the exception to the rule – we'd been one of the 98 per cent after all. We were together for eighteen years, and I have my wonderful children to remind me that there were good times. Splitting just after our wedding anniversary should have been more symbolic than it was really; instead, it was just one little thing after another. I'm still locking everything away, but that will just have to do because life isn't kind enough to give you space to look at things, you just have to keep plodding on.

Dad came back for one thing, though.

He came back for the birth of your little sister, Ellie.

Well, he was around, but not really present in a funny way. I think he was just going through the motions.

She is so beautiful — and so, so like you, my darling. I had a home birth; I don't think hospitals are the right place and I think it's a natural process that we should try and keep that way. My fifth baby, my fifth child. My body is used to it by now, and I gave birth on my own, easily. I have a body that knows how to do this and childbirth just isn't that painful for me. Anyway, it's pain for the right reasons and I can't complain about that. Giving birth is just a process really and I'd have a hundred babies if I could. Ellie was late but it all went well, perfectly really. I think, even if I had found it hard, the PTSD would have helped in a funny way because I can lock pain away.

I keep going back to how much she resembles you — it's uncanny.

But I need to block all of that out. It's unfair on both of you but it's worse for her; she can't start life being compared to you. From the moment she was born, people wanted to make comparisons, but I can't have that. It is going to be a strange world for little Ellie. The world already knows her two big sisters, the one who is here and the one who isn't.

Charlotte has been brilliant with her from the start, soothing her and helping out. If you had been here, I wouldn't have got a look in between the two of you! Yes, someone is missing, but there is a new life to celebrate. Ellie is her own person but she does have a sister that the whole world knows apart from her, and we'll all have to find a way through that. I think this might help Charlotte find her way too – she's the big sister now and it's a completely new role for her. She never leaves my side, she still needs me so much, and I do wonder whether there will be enough of me to go round soon. Before Ellie arrived, I was still carrying Charlotte everywhere, even though she's nine now, so I wonder how she'll cope with that, with the baby needing to be carried instead of her.

Sometimes, I feel guilty I've had another baby, that I have moved on. In the few weeks after Ellie was born, I did have the baby blues. Any time I took her out in the pram, Charlotte would put a blanket over the hood so that no one could see her. I'm obsessively protective, and so is she. She is a wonderful big sister. I'm still sleeping very badly, but when I do finally manage, it's as if I'm in a coma. If Ellie needs me, Charlotte will always be there to wake me up and tell me, or she's already brought her to me for feeding. I think Lee and Luke are a bit scared of her, to be honest. I guess boys of sixteen and fourteen don't have that much interest in babies, but I do wonder if they're also a bit scared to connect in case they lose her too? They are there for us though, I do know that. Sometimes I feel as if Charlotte and I are her parents, as your dad is so removed; not just physically, emotionally too.

2003

Ellie is wonderful but she hasn't stopped the flashbacks. In fact, my PTSD has been worse since she's been born. I keep seeing your life as film clips almost, the images fast forward from when you were born to when you were a toddler to when you were five years old to when . . . Well, the usual nightmares kick in then. It's as if everything flashes at once, as if I'm seeing lots of screens, and it's terrifying.

Will you help me keep her safe, princess, will you? Please? Surely we deserve a bit of luck, just a little bit, so if you can throw some of your angel dust down here to protect little Ellie — to protect all of your brothers and sisters — then that would be the most magical thing.

This is hard, darling — I love you so much. xx

2004

DARLING SARAH —

I had forgotten just how the time passes when you have a new baby. Every day seems to be the same for a while, but then I look at her, and see that she's growing, see that she's changing, and I think *I did that!* It's so lovely to have a baby in my arms — I never feel better than when I'm being a mum. I'm tired, but I was tired before Ellie got here — it's just for a wonderful reason now. I have five children, *five*, and all of you have such different characters. This one is feisty already: she gathers her hands into little fists when she doesn't get what she wants quickly enough, and she has Charlotte fussing over her the whole time.

She has been good for all of us. There is nothing more beautiful than the gurgle of a newborn, and sometimes

I just snuggle into her, sniffing that baby smell and wondering how something so perfect came from the mess of your dad and me. I can't help but think how you would have been as her biggest sister. You would have loved her to bits, there's no doubt about that, and you would have told her stories, stroked her fat little cheeks, helped me bathe and dress her. I tell her about you all the time, and I swear she listens intently. She will grow up knowing you and not knowing you. She will hear all about her famous big sister, the one who has helped so many children through her name being at the forefront of a campaign that puts their safety first – the sister whose loss has meant that other little ones will be saved,, but she will never have the pleasure of knowing you in her day-to-day life. I wonder if she would even be here if we hadn't lost you; if Dad and I would have stumbled along, would we have separated anyway, would we have made Ellie?

Too many questions … none of them will ever be answered. I need to just live in the moment, live with what I've got. I don't think any mother who has a baby after losing a child can be prepared for the onslaught of feelings. The happiness is tinged with guilt – should I be cuddling another little girl? Should I be happy with her when you're not here? You can think about it in advance until you make yourself sick with thinking, but the reality can't be planned. The emotions can change from one second to the next. I'm angry when people don't mention you when they meet her for the first time, then I'm angry if they do and I think it detracts from Ellie as her own person. The PTSD helps to some extent – I can box things up, but it rips me apart on other days. I worry I won't be enough for her, then I worry I'll smother her with my love.

And life doesn't really give you a break. There's barely time to catch your breath before something else comes along. Nanny had been staying with us over Christmas this year and everything was fine, she was delighted with Ellie, but when she went home after New Year, things took a turn for the worse. As she got out of the car, she fell and broke her hip. That was the start of a whole spiral of events that has left me shattered. You know how close I was to my mum – she gave me my values, she showed me how to have a family, and she was a rock when we lost you. However, when she went to hospital to have her hip mended, they found something much worse: Nanny had lung cancer. Within five weeks, by February, she was dead, Sarah.

I can't quite believe it: my strong, loving, wonderful mother – gone. In those last weeks I took little Ellie with me to Kent to look after Mum; Michael and friends looked after the other children. You just go where you're needed, or at least, I do. I was battered and I was numb – again. It was one thing after another. I'm not the only one, though. Plenty of people have bad lives, but I do wonder how any of us cope. I said to you before that there is no manual for grief, there is no rulebook about how you are meant to cope when you lose a child, but the same is true when you lose a parent. It doesn't matter that I'm a grown woman with children of my own – I want my mum. I want her to hold me and tell me everything will be fine, I want her to stroke my hair and tell me that she loves me. I want to make her proud and I want her to be there forever. I just want time to stand still, really. I want what I had – I want you and I want Mum, but I want Ellie too. I want what I can't have – don't we all?

Sometimes I wonder what I must have done in a previous life though. I loosely believe in reincarnation, I suppose, and I definitely believe in karma, that's why I refuse to have hate in my life, but why all of this? I try to be a good person, and I think I am, so why all of this heartache? I really do hope I had an absolutely brilliant time in a previous life to have to pay so much in this one – if only I could remember it!

I was with Mum when she died. I could hardly bear to say goodbye but I knew that she needed to be released, she needed to be free of the pain. There can't be a family in the world who hasn't been touched by cancer and I bet we all feel the same way – the selfishness of wanting to keep your loved one with you for as long as possible, knowing every second is agony for them. I knew she had to go, I knew I had to let her go, and I was just grateful that she had met Ellie. As soon as I left the hospital, I knew there was one thing I had to do: I had to write a dedication for the book I'd been working on, to acknowledge Mum. It was for her – the woman who had made me who I am.

Mum had adored you, Sarah, you knew that – she was

from an era where you got on with things, but burying a youngster hit her hard. How do you bury your own, she had once asked me, and I had to say I didn't know. She had always thought I would be a writer so it's such a shame she didn't live to see my book. Not long after she died, it topped all the bestseller lists, my darling, and the reaction was so positive. She would have loved that; she would have been bursting with pride at what her little girl had achieved, just as I burst with pride when I think of you. We are a family of strong women, Sarah, and Nanny's memory will drive me on, just as yours does.

I'd cut back on Sarah's Law when I was pregnant with Ellie – it went on the backburner for a while so I could be at home. I try not to think of Ellie's twin, of the baby I lost. I try very hard to concentrate on what I have, not what might have been, but I also pulled back a little just in case working so hard had been a factor in losing the little one.

Roy Whiting has had an appeal this year. It didn't really involve me – it's a paperwork exercise, really. I think he will probably keep appealing until there isn't a breath left in his body. It doesn't matter to him; it passes the time. Does he enjoy the idea that he is pushing himself into our thoughts again?

It's easy for them, for prisoners, to launch appeals as they get legal aid. He's not that intelligent, he goes with the flow. Lawyers get publicity for such a well-known case and he agrees to it all. I wonder how they sleep at night, though. The lawyers who advised him that it's worth appealing, knowing full well that, if they succeed, he'll be out on the streets again. He won't change – paedophiles don't. Have they thought about that? Have they thought about what they would be releasing if they won? I guess it's just their job, but what a job! What a way to live.

We knew that the conviction would always be challenged – he was one of the last tariffs imposed by Home Secretary David Blunkett. I felt that we had got rid of capital punishment to put life imprisonment in place and it was absolutely right that there was a tariff. However, not everyone agreed with me, and with that disagreement came the possibility of appeal after appeal. But I couldn't give in to my emotions when it happened; if I did, I'd go down – I'd drown. I know that I haven't dealt with things: I couldn't do it then, and I can't do it now: maybe one day, maybe not.

A friend asked me when the appeal was going on, 'How do you deal with it, Sara? How do you deal with seeing his face every time you turn on the news?'

'He's nothing,' I told her. 'He's nothing to me. He doesn't even register.'

'But . . . he took Sarah. Doesn't that just make you hate him so much?'

I've explained this to many, many people over and over again, but I think I'll be explaining forever.

'It was just as likely to be Sarah as any other little girl. He's said that. He said he was looking, and it was just luck – good luck for him, awful luck for her – that she was there.

Why would I think we were immune to that? Why would I think it should be someone else's child? All I know is that I can't let him get me as well. I can't let myself be consumed by hate, because if I allow that, then he really has won.'

There has been so much in the news this year, so many things happening, and it all makes me think of you. When Blunkett resigned in December, I knew that would have an impact, not just on Whiting's appeal, but on Sarah's Law too as I would have to wait and see whether we would be supported or opposed. Maxine Carr was released and the whole circus around Holly Wells and Jessica Chapman started up again. There was a tsunami which killed thousands and made me think of the fragility of life, as always, and, in the middle of it all, Ellie had her first birthday.

With Lee and Luke and Charlotte I've been working hard to protect her since the day she was born, and I think you have too, Sarah. Charlotte is still very cautious about her baby sister and hates people leaning into her. She's not got much memory of the time when you were taken, but like me, she does have PTSD – they all do. When the other kids went to school after you were taken, they would often come back very upset – they would repeat what their parents had been saying and for me that was a wake-up call really, to know what people thought behind closed doors.

Lee once told me that he'd been bullied for not saving you, and that kids were coming into school, repeating things they had heard at home. Cruel words which said it was all our fault, that we were to blame; that we deserved to lose you because we weren't looking after you properly. Some people said we were more interested in being at the pub than looking after our children; some said we were neglectful and that Sarah was better off away from us. They said these things within earshot of their own children – they must have done, because these children then brought such hateful words to school and taunted my boys with them. Children wouldn't have come up with these things themselves: it was the cruelty of their parents.

It hurt. Of course it hurt, and it made your brothers so angry. I had tried to prepare them for this sort of thing but it was worse than I'd thought – anyway, how can you prepare your children for the cruel words of adults, adults who would say that we were to blame? Their children would say, you were with her, you were there; you should have stopped it from happening, and I hadn't really told the boys they might hear things as horrible as that.

We had a small party for Ellie but it was difficult as I think we're having trouble connecting and I'm really feeling the loss of my mum. No one loves your kids like your mum does. You had been the first girl for a long time, princess, and Mum was over the moon when you were born. Now, I have another little baby girl but I don't have my mum to share her with. There are too many gaps in my life, but I have to focus on the gifts too, and that's exactly what Ellie is in my life. I have to fight – I can't drown. I can't give up. These children, this family, need me and I will never let them down.

Christmas is always hard – Christmas Day especially. I have

a few quiet tears, no screaming. Screaming isn't really my thing. New Year's Eve is the same. *Swim, don't sink*, that's what I tell myself. Just keep breathing, in and out; one foot in front of the other, all the clichés … it's worth it. Life doesn't necessarily get better, but when the worst has happened, what else can go wrong? I could get wrapped up in the bad but I have five amazing children; I've done a pretty good job. I just wish there was someone who would tell me that – I'd like to hear those words from someone who loves me.

The thing about grief is that, just when you think you are over the worst, it rears its head in the most unexpected of places to remind you that you'll never quite be free. It's always there, just waiting.

Whether it's Christmas, or a birthday, or Mother's Day, I know there are other families across the country, and they are normal. They are untouched; they give each other cards and bubble-bath sets and novelty mugs, and they get on with life. I get on with life too, we all do, but there is always something lurking, always the loss, waiting, waiting to catch us. There's an empty chair where you would be, a plate that isn't smothered in ketchup. Gifts I haven't bought for you; a handmade card I haven't received from you. Every space a reminder it should all be so very different.

I don't think I'll ever come to terms with the circumstances of your death, but I don't think I'll ever get over losing my mum or my brother either. Sometimes I wonder about how broken everyone is. All the people I walk past on the street, every neighbour, every person on

TV … We all suffer quietly, we all carry the scars of the losses we bear.

I feel the loss of you all the time, but it is when it catches me unaware, when I can't breathe for the fact you aren't here, that it physically hurts. When I watch a film you loved, or see a book you adored. When I buy that ketchup or read a fairy tale – you're there! But you're not.

I'm still working to make you proud, and I will get back on that horse once Ellie's a little older, and I will spend the rest of my life making sure none of this was in vain. I'll keep trying to be happy; I'll never stop loving. I'll always do what I can to make the most of the life I am blessed to still have, because it was denied to you and I don't have the right to waste it. That's all I have left to give you, and I can only hope it's enough.

There's no hierarchy of grief. You can't know how much someone means to someone else; you can't know how big the gap is, what they've lost. People grieve at their own pace, mourning doesn't stick to a set of rules that we can all follow – but wouldn't that be lovely? It's eighteen months so I feel better. It's three years so I can laugh again without feeling guilty. It's ten years, so I'm actually 'fixed' now. No, that's not how life, or death, goes on.

It's subjective.

It's unique to everyone.

But we all hurt like hell, I know that much.

When I think back to all of those cuddly toys that were sent and left for you, I'm still overwhelmed by the sheer number. Someone asked me recently how I felt about it, how I felt about so many people mourning you at the same time as me. I'm not sure I felt much back then – I was just surviving. But now, when I reflect, I can see that people felt they were really just saying 'We're thinking of you', they were grieving too. Even though most of them hadn't known you, there had been such a pulling together of the whole country when you went missing, and then when the search happened, that I can understand how so many felt a connection had been made.

I spoke about you in such detail – there were all of those days when I thought you'd be found, when I thought you'd just walk through the door, and I had to keep you alive in the minds of every single person who might be able to help. I didn't know who that might be – I didn't know who might have seen you, who might still be seeing you; if you were somewhere you could be heard or whether you were walking around, whether you'd lost your memory, or someone had been on holiday and was only just catching up with the news. Maybe they'd be the one. I had to hope; I had to keep trying, and so, I guess, what also happened was that the rest of the country – the rest of the world – became invested in my princess too. When you were found, when I had to face up to the loss of you, so did they. Is it any wonder they needed to do something; they needed to show that it mattered?

Because it did, Sarah.

It mattered so very much.

You weren't just my lost little angel any more: you were a symbol of everything that was wrong with how children are treated and abused in our culture. Of how victims are second-class citizens, and how the rights of offenders are always put first.

Sending me a teddy bear or laying down a stuffed toy animal at our front door would change nothing in itself, but the sheer numbers showed me that I had an army behind me. And that army was what powered me on. They were showing respect for you and for what I would have to do, and I had a duty to make sure something was achieved as a result of your death and their loss as well as my own.

Am I distancing myself when I think that way? Maybe. Who knows? PTSD works in funny ways, just as grief does. I can sometimes see myself, as if I'm watching someone else, and I can analyse quite clearly why I'm reacting the way I am. Other times, I barely know what day it is when I think of all that's happened.

I know I should be happy – and I am, I'm happy that I have a healthy child – but there always seems to be a price for any good thing.

The price is a heavy one. My mum has passed away and I don't know how much more of this I can take. Your Uncle Paul dying last year when I found out I was pregnant with Ellie, and now your nanny this year. I know that I'm locking everything away, but what else can I do? Life isn't kind enough to give you time to look at things, it just throws one thing after another at you and says *here you go, cope with this now!*

I'm coping – I am, but I need you to get me through, princess. Don't let me drown. xx

2005

MY WONDERFUL GIRL —

I have met someone who I think will change my life. And
not just my life — the lives of so many others too. A woman
called Shy Keenan has come into my life, and I just know
that she will be a wonderful friend and a fantastic ally in
the battle to make children safe. When we started talking,
we immediately clicked. She was working on a tagging
project which interested me as part of Sarah's Law and I
knew she would be a good friend from the start, I just felt
that connection. What I love is that there is no previous
link between her and the old me, she just knows me as I
am now; there's no baggage, there's no Sara before-you
and after-you with her. She just sees me as the woman I
am today.

Shy is fierce, Sarah! She works in child protection and has been watching the work I've been doing, the changes I want to make, and she is so supportive. Talking to her makes me realise how much I've actually done in such a short period of time and it allows me to feel proud. She makes me see that it's me doing it all and I think I needed that recognition. She's a fighter, a whirlwind, so very strong. We're going to make a great team, but what a life she's had.

I knew of her book before I met her and the start of it had always stuck with me – *I was born and broken in Birkenhead.* And, by God, was she broken. As a tiny little girl she had been abused by a network of paedophiles in every way possible. Shy had been abused and photographed, told it was love, told it should hurt, and every hideous thing in between. She was hit, sold, left for dead, and deserted. No one ever seemed to give any thought to what sort of woman that abused child would become, but she has grown into someone who has taken every horror thrown at her and used it to fight for good. Miraculously, she survived it all.

The thing is, Sarah, Shy told people. She told people then and she wasn't believed. And, today, even now, the same thing is happening: children tell and they aren't believed. How can it still be going on? Why hasn't it been stopped? Is it because our society doesn't really want to stop it? I don't want that to be the case, but until I've fought with every last breath in my body to help the victims, then I will always believe there is hope.

Like me, Shy feels that being a mother is all about love, that it is easy to love your children, easy to be swept up in how much they mean to you — but we both have to accept that isn't the case for everyone. There are women as well as men who abuse, and there are women who turn a blind eye to it too. The only thing that matters is the victim; we both know that, and now that we have found each other, we can fight for it even more.

Shy's had such bad stuff happen to her but she's also made the decision to be a good person. Those were choices I made too: you don't get the right to be bad because bad things happened to you. I have a dark gallows humour, a sarcasm that gets me through, and she gets that and makes me laugh. With her I can be the new me — whatever that is. I don't have to hide anything from her, she reads me like a book. We'd laugh at the stupidity of the system. She made me stronger, a bit prouder; she came into my life just when I needed her. We're both formidable forces but she sees when I'm hiding things from her. She'll say — *you'll feel the way you feel*. I like that. Maybe I needed permission to feel this way; maybe I needed it from someone who understands all of this.

There was a General Election in May of this year, which means that I will again have to deal with new politicians in new roles who will often fight against what I want; but Shy will be on my side this time. I don't feel that people are against making changes for victims of abuse as such, I just feel they aren't used to someone like me making such a noise about it.

What they have to realise is this: I won't go away.

Ever.

I will keep shouting about this, and I will keep fighting for it until things change. Your memory will always be enough to keep me doing those things – it's not as if I'm going to wake up one day and say, *how fantastic – everything's sorted now!* I know that it will never be sorted, but it can be a hell of a lot better than it is at the moment.

Grief makes you a shell of the person you were before, Sarah. It would be so easy to let all of the bad things win, but I'm trying to be positive, I really am. Each day I struggle but we're not in this world for long, so I'm doing what I can to make the most of it and make it better for other people. I wish I could tell everyone to make the most of their loved ones, to not waste time on petty things; to live for the day. Sometimes I feel that I bounce back pretty well – sometimes I feel there's a little less of me every time. We all need to be kinder, more forgiving, to judge less and understand more. We all go through grief alone, it's our personal path to walk, but with that kindness in the world, things can be a little more bearable.

I lost a part of me when I lost you, darling, but I have learned a lot too. When someone dies, and when you have loved that someone very much, there is no rulebook as to what you will feel. I knew that when I lost you, but now that Nanny and your uncle have gone as well, I feel as if I've had to relearn it. If only there *was* a pattern to follow. Maybe it would be more bearable if you knew that it would all be the worst it could be on Day One, then as time progressed there would be a little lifting of the agony. It doesn't, though – it doesn't work like that at all. You get good days but then you wonder, was it good because I didn't think about her so much, or because I did? Then you get bad days – but then you think, how dare I think any day *isn't* bad when she isn't here?

Some days I'm at peace with my losses, other days I feel as if I'm drowning (*don't drown, Sara, don't drown, don't give in, don't sink, keep fighting*). I think the most important thing I've learned is that there is no rhyme or reason to any of this, it just is. I can't keep looking for answers, because there aren't any. I can't change what has happened, I can't get any of you back. All I can do is be here for Luke and Lee and Charlotte and Ellie, and hope against all hope that I will always be strong enough to make up for the fact that they have had to deal with all of this simply because I'm their mother.

But I am.

Like every mother who deserves the name, I am the glue that holds this family together and I will fight until my last breath to keep us in one piece.

And, do you know what, Sarah?

Sometimes the light comes from places you don't even expect.

Do you remember Mole? Probably not. He's an old

friend of mine; someone I've known since I was a child. You did meet him – very briefly, it maybe didn't even register. But, somehow, we've found each other again and, princess, finally I feel there is someone who will take care of me. I need that so much. When things went wrong between me and your dad – or when I accepted that they had been wrong for a very long time and they would never be fixed – it was painful. Yes, I'm strong; yes, I'm a fighter, but I still want to be held and loved and looked after. Doesn't everyone?

I had decided I would be on my own forever. Things had been so hard with your dad – and they still are; we still fight and we still hurt each other – but then, slowly, things changed in the most unexpected way. Mole and I were seeing each other so often, and he was confiding in me as his own relationship fell apart, then, all at once we realised that something was happening! It was careful and tentative, but slowly and surely, something started to build. It was a bit like one of your fairy tales, darling – you know that part in *Beauty and the Beast* where Belle starts to wonder what's going on? She sings about there being 'something there that wasn't there before' – well, we're no Disney story, but I think that is almost how it was for us. It isn't without its complications – what is? – but worth working on, worth fighting for. We'd had a loose friendship but I had decided I would always be on my own. Over the past few years we'd all accepted your dad was an alcoholic and there were such frightening highs and lows when I was with him, which only got worse over time. I started to see Mole and my life moved on just a little more.

I knew this was painful for your dad. For me it was cautious and tentative but slowly and surely it started to work. I was never brave enough to tell your dad straight to his face that we would never get back together again – I always hoped he would sort himself out and I really did all I could, but it was clear there was no more, we were done. I was angry with him that he'd fallen apart when I had kept it together, when the other children had kept it together too. The boys had gone through more than us, in my eyes, so why was he so weak? Why could he not even put a public face on it any more? He was drunk all the time; he was having fights with people and it was beginning to tarnish your memory. He had his demons – I want to be honest about him without being brutal, Sarah, but I've always been so angry that he hadn't the strength to be what he needed to be for your memory, my darling.

I've actually known Mole since I was twelve or thirteen – about the age you would be now if you were with us. We had our whole lives ahead of us; who could have guessed we would meet up now, after so much has happened, after so much that life has thrown in our way? I didn't even know that I needed what he gives me, Sarah. It's an easy relationship; close and straightforward. I know that you would have been devastated about me splitting with your dad, but it was for the best, and this is for the best too. Mole is kind and he makes me stronger – I feel like I can lean on him and I love the fact that he has strong morals. Being able to rely on someone is like a breath of fresh air. With your dad I was always the stronger personality but this relationship is old-fashioned and easy. We danced around each other for a while before I spoke to your brothers and Charlotte (Ellie was too little to know what was going on, really), and I waited a while until it felt right. I've found it so difficult to trust and to believe in someone else's strength because toxic has been my normality. I wonder if meeting Shy has helped – she's allowed me to see that there are people who can be trusted, and maybe she's the one who changed me in that way, so that I could even consider letting Mole in.

I thought I'd be on my own forever and I was happy with that – or at least I'd accepted it. I don't think I knew how much I needed someone until now. Dad has been diagnosed as bipolar and his depression is getting worse. He was in hospital for some weeks after your death, but now he's getting more and more erratic. I really don't know what the future holds for him. When I think back to how we were, when we were young and made all of our plans for our family, he seems like a different person. Roy Whiting has broken him, but he'll never break me, I won't allow that. Even though we're divorced and really don't have that much to do with each other, I still want your dad to have a good life, Sarah – I'm just not sure that will ever happen.

*

It's been quite a year, princess – new friend, new love, and I really do believe that attitudes are beginning to change about what we can do to protect our children as well. I'm getting used to working with politicians and the government, but I feel the key to all of this is about changing hearts as well as minds, in the system and in law enforcement.

Police officers are dealing with this every day and what I want to say to them is that Sarah's Law can help them: it wouldn't be there to make things harder and it certainly wouldn't give them more work. It would give some power back to ordinary people, to parents; it would mean that if you had a suspicion, if you just had a gut feeling that something wasn't quite right, you would have the ability to check on that. Most of the time nothing would come of it, but if there was something there – well, the police could work together with a community to make sure that all of the children there were safe. Isn't that what everyone wants?

I have such confidence in this. It is 100 per cent the right thing to do and there's no doubt in my mind that it needs to be implemented. Sometimes I'm surprised that I make so much sense and they are lacking in it! I'm just an ordinary mum and they are the ones who are meant to be so clever, so on top of everything, but they're completely lacking in common sense. They have no idea of normal lives. I had always been told by your grandparents that manners would get you far in life and it's true. We can disagree and debate but I will never stoop low – I will always be respectful and I will always listen to their arguments, but I would always hope that I could change their minds on things that matter too.

There is always a lot of talk about the death penalty – people are surprised I don't support it, but I say this to them: how can I put that on you? How can I place such a huge burden on you? They don't know how to answer that. Usually it's the same people who say, who have been saying since the start, 'I wouldn't survive if it happened to me,' but I did, and sometimes, I even smiled. Was I wrong? You have to live while you're grieving. I do laugh but not on the inside, not really. When you were missing and we begged for you to come home, I made a conscious effort to say, 'if Sarah is watching,' so I'd been putting on a brave face then and I won't change that; I'll put on a brave face whenever it's required. The cameras will never get my grief and neither will he. Grief sometimes catches me unawares, usually in the middle of something so normal, like when we're all sitting round the dinner table and I suddenly miss you with every part of me, or a memory comes out of nowhere. It can catch your breath; it can knock you for six. If someone ever notices though, I brush it away.

Here's a secret between us – I'm nowhere near as strong as I make out. It's easy to pretend to be strong. I've had next to no counselling. It would have made it worse back then – too painful, I wouldn't have been able to speak openly about that day. I don't want ifs and buts, but who knows now? Maybe it was just meant to be – maybe that was your destiny and this is mine. I always had a sense that I wouldn't have you for long, you were so precious. I always thought that I wouldn't see you through to adulthood. I didn't get that feeling at all with the others. Once it happened, once you'd gone, the memory of that came flooding back. I'd forgotten it. A friend who had kids the same age, with whom I had walked to school, remembered me saying it. I think I did sense it: something was going to happen.

I'm not saying I was ever psychic, I don't believe in that sort of thing, but there was a sense that you just wouldn't be with me for as long as you should be. It wasn't a premonition. Oh, it's so hard to explain this, sweetheart. It wasn't as if I had a vision that you would die, and I certainly never thought of how you it would happen, it was just a feeling. I could never imagine you as an adult. I could never see you in the future as a grown woman, as a mother with children of her own. It wasn't as if every time I looked at you there was sadness – far from it, you filled me with joy. You were a shining light who brought such happiness to everyone you met. It was as if there was a glow that shone out from inside your heart. Too much, too much to bear … Your kindness, your innocence, they just seemed as if they would be too much for a cruel world. It's a cliché, but I did have a belief that you were too good for all of this. I don't know how you would have coped with the bad things that are around us, even if you had never been taken that day, even if you'd lived a so-called normal life.

And yet you would have been just the sort of person this world needs. Had you stayed, I think you would have done so many wonderful things: you would have fought for the people who need a warrior, for children, for the oppressed, but for you what would the cost have been? I always thought you'd help children, and it turns out you've been the greatest child protector ever. My princess, you died in the most horrendous way possible but there's a little balance in what we are doing together that makes it a little bit easier to live with.

Wish me luck – not just with life now, but with love as well. xx

2006

There was a heatwave this summer, darling, which took me back to those boiling hot days of six years ago. It was as if the whole country had slowed down, but I couldn't. I never can. There's so much to do, so many people to see, so much to try and put in place. I could never have imagined my life would be like this — not just a life without you, but one where I'm constantly speaking to important people, to government officials, to police and politicians. I just try to remember who I am, to ground myself, and remember the little girl who made all of this possible.

I wonder what you think of me, looking down, seeing all of this? It's all for you but I sometimes worry that you're forgotten in the midst of everything. That can never happen – I'll never allow it to happen, but for other people there isn't that terror that one day, the Sarah who started all of this won't be remembered any more. When we started the campaign, Sarah's Law and For Sarah, there was never any question that you wouldn't be at the forefront of it, but as time goes on, I suppose there will be people who don't remember that day and maybe they'll suggest there are other names, different titles, that should be used. I'll never allow that; I'll never allow you to be forgotten, darling. You are a beacon of light for all abused children, and for the changes that need to be made. It will all be done in your name and no one will ever forget you.

There is a new home secretary, a man called John Reid, who I think will be our ally. He seems practical, realistic – I think he's willing to find out what all of this is about and look at what really needs to be done. A lot of people say he's a bit of a battlehorse but I feel that he's really on our side – I'm comfortable with him. He doesn't make me feel inferior or uneducated, he listens and acknowledges there are things I know, things that British people feel and that politicians haven't done anything about for years. He seems like his own man and he knows the value of having principles.

Do you remember what I said at the first appeal when you were missing, darling? I said we were a strong family and that we don't survive well apart. Now I'm having to survive, Sarah, we all are – but there are cracks, so many cracks. The most horrible thing happened when there was a 'sorry' note found at your grave, signed with the initials of the man who took you. It wasn't him, of course it wasn't him – he's locked up. Some sick bastard thought that it would be funny, or maybe they hoped to hurt us even more. Whoever it was didn't just have their sights on us – notes like it were left with flowers on the graves of Holly Wells and Jessica Chapman too. Those were meant to be from Ian Huntley. It was absolutely disgusting. Whoever did it desecrated the graves of all of you. I can't imagine what kind of sick individual would do such a thing. I was so upset and wanted to get to the bottom of it, but I also didn't want to give any attention to whoever had done it in the first place, as I know that's just what they would have wanted.

The Home Office had to put out a statement and said any suggestion that the flowers and notes had been sent by the jailed killers was 'utterly untrue. As far as we are concerned, any allegation that either prisoner had anything to do with it is utterly untrue. We totally refute it.' But we saw the pictures, we saw them in the newspapers, and they ripped us apart. There was a white card attached to white and pink roses by Holly's Soham grave. It read: 'To Holly rest in peace Ian'. A similar note was left on Jessica's grave, whereas the one for you read: 'To Sarah Sorry RW'. It was wrapped around a bunch of white roses and it was completely twisted.

I don't want it to take away from the huge successes we have had this year. Along with our friends at the *News of the*

World, we have seen one of the major achievements in our battle – a day I often wondered about, a day I sometimes thought I'd never see. Sarah's Law, *your* law, my darling, is on the brink of being introduced. It's been a long fight, but John Reid is the man who has finally seen sense. He is wonderfully practical and seems to know what is right, and finally, finally, he has ordered a complete review of the campaign with a view to implementing your law in Britain. Can you imagine it, princess? We're almost there.

Not only has John said yes, we need to do this, but he has started to look at why so much is being done to help offenders, while victims suffer. He has closed eleven bail hostels to sex offenders and said it's just the beginning. We have been fighting about that for so long, because many of these hostels are right next to schools and surely no one in their right mind can argue that paedophiles should be placed there.

Without any fanfare, John Reid did it: he closed the hostels to them. Then he moved sixty abusers away from areas where they were close to vulnerable kids. He sent one of his team to America to learn about Megan's Law, the US version of what I want to see here, and he did so without drawing any attention to himself, vowing that parents would be entitled to much more information about paedophiles in their area. Megan was a seven-year-old from New Jersey who had been raped and murdered by her neighbour, Jesse Timmendequas, after he lured her to his house. He already had convictions for sexually assaulting two other little girls, and one of the experts involved in his case said she always believed he would do it again. A month after Megan's murder, the New Jersey General Assembly passed a series of bills which would require sex offender registry and a database of names. Communities would be notified when an offender moved into their area and repeat offenders would be jailed for life. Megan's Law was brought in federally in 1996 to help children, to protect them – it was too late for Megan, and it's too late for you, but there should never be another child who suffers because we are too afraid to pass the laws this country needs.

This was such a change in attitude from someone at the very heart of British government. It sent shock waves through the entire system when he said, 'I start from the position that information should no longer remain the exclusive preserve of officialdom.' Some journalists were actually a bit put out by all of this – they are so used to politicians making a song and dance about every little thing they do, they were almost offended that John had done so much. It's unheard of for a top-level minister to send one of his most senior ranking officials on a fact-finding mission without the need to have his back patted and be told how wonderful he is. I guess it sells newspapers and generates articles, so they missed out when he simply announced that it was done, that he had already set the ball rolling. He said, 'We will go to America to see how it's done there and look hard at the Sarah's Law proposals.'

Some people might say that's his cop out if he needs one – he's only said he will 'look hard', but I believe he is genuine and he has principles. I think he'll do this, Sarah. He says that he wants to study specifically what I have worked on with Rebekah Wade at the *News of the World*, and that he is particularly interested in whether members of the public, ordinary people, should be given controlled access to information. He was quoted as saying, 'I believe the public have the right to protection and they have the right to information. We must make sure that we get the balance right though and that the free flow of information does not undermine the public's safety.' It's what I've been waiting to hear for six years.

It was such a huge breakthrough in the For Sarah campaign, but I guess they just couldn't keep fobbing us off any longer. We have battled for so long, relentlessly; we have confronted the Home Office with evidence for those six years. They have been given the material showing how many newly released paedophiles are put into local communities without people ever knowing their children are at risk, and now John Reid has said that just won't happen. He has promised no child sex offenders will stay in accommodation directly adjacent to schools. Do you know something? When he announced that, even though there is still so much to do, I swear I slept that night. For me, that is an achievement as huge as anything else.

For them to also look at Megan's Law in detail means things really are moving. Megan's Law was the first to publish details of where paedophiles were living, and it was the inspiration behind everything. John Reid's official on this, junior minister Gerry Sutcliffe, has said that he wants children to be given the maximum amount of protection possible. This is wonderful to hear, but what sort of world are we living in where we don't already have that? At what point was it decided that children and their safety should be placed at the bottom of the pile? It was as if, at last, a change in the attitude of the department was bringing them into line with what I'd been saying for years, and what the British public supported. The mum of Megan Kanka agreed, and when she heard what was happening, said, 'The only way to keep children safe is for stronger laws.' But Megan's Law isn't the only one – there is a change coming. Jessica's Law has also been introduced in the US after a nine-year-old girl, Jessica Lunsford, was abducted, raped and buried alive in February 2005. How can we protect the people who do these things, those who fantasise about carrying out such crimes, but leave children without protection? How can anyone justify that?

Normal people going about their normal lives haven't seen what I've seen, Sarah – and I don't want them to. I want them to get on with ordinary things, like watching the World Cup this summer (we miss you for things like that, for joining in with us all when we get excited, and for playing with our dog Fifa when it all gets too much for him!). They shouldn't know about the dark things; they should be able to rely on those they elect to protect them as much as possible. I'm just an ordinary mum, but I will do all I can to make sure that the darkness is beaten by the light. You are my light and you will shine brighter than anything else, my love.

Not everyone agrees with me, of course. I met another man this year who thinks I'm wrong – a man called Lord Falconer, who was at a victims' conference in Newcastle. I didn't take to him one little bit. He is quite aloof, as if emotion has no part in all of this. He thinks Sarah's Law is nonsense and this angered me so much – how dare he! Most politicians have such entrenched thinking and only want to take on the non-emotional side; they want findings and figures, most of them apart from John Reid, that is. Well, here's a figure for them – there are 2 million strong and good and angry British citizens behind me, and we won't be silenced any longer.

I genuinely can't see how people can ignore the evidence. Earlier this year, there was an organisation set up which proves how much needs to be done and how much can be done with the right approach. Called the Child Exploitation & Online Protection Centre (CEOP), it's headed by a man called Jim Gamble who used to be the Deputy Director General of the National Crime Squad (now the National Crime Agency). Their work is so important – they are bringing together law enforcement officers, specialists from children's charities and computer experts to work together and change things. There is now a 24/7 online resource dedicated to report online child sexual abuse; also systems in place to track sex offenders and send the intelligence they discover to a global network of child protection support teams. They will work on identifying children who have been victims of child sexual abuse and push them towards help; they will work on domestic and international raids on paedophiles too. And they will work in schools to teach children about online safety and be part of a global alliance with Canada, the US, Australia and Interpol. They will develop specialist training services and work constantly to change the culture that harms children. The Home Office said, when CEOP was set up in April 2006, that child sexual abuse was one of the worst crimes imaginable; that victims were attacked during their most vulnerable years and often the effects lasted a lifetime. With this sort of statement, I can't see why anyone wouldn't want to be fighting that fight too, rather than saying I was wrong.

Jim Gamble said:'Let us be clear. If you are a sex offender, get help or get caught. The internet will increasingly expose you to new policing powers and will cease to be the anonymous place that it once was.' This was music to my ears, and within weeks the CEOP had snared its first online grooming offender. It's part of the puzzle, part of the network we need, and a sign that there is an army ready to battle this cancer in our society.

Grief is a strange thing. It can lull you in, make you think you're coping, and then, just as you feel maybe things will be OK, it stabs you. The loss. The *lack* of you, Sarah – sometimes, the actual physical lack of you is so very painful. So, I fall. Sometimes, and never when anyone else can see me, but sometimes I do fall into it.

We've made such strides this year: we've worked with good people and it's finally seemed as if there's progress – then, WHAM! It's back. The emptiness. Not being able to sleep. Seeing the empty chair at the dinner table. Seeing the image of the eight-year-old you who will never grow up.

There are other times when I think, this is just life. People cope with terrible things all the time. Can I say my loss is greater than someone whose child died of cancer? Or someone who is living with the knowledge that their child *will* die of cancer? What about a mother who waves her child off to school in the morning and then gets a call to say the trip they have been on has ended in a coach crash? Then there's the woman who loses a baby to cot death, or to stillbirth, or to miscarriage. Where do we draw the line if we start thinking like that? Do we say, 'Here you are – your grief is much bigger, much worse, than the person next to you, so you will get more sympathy, you can grieve for six months longer'. Do we start to measure how much that child was lost?

What of the woman who loses her husband of sixty years? Is that worse than the newlywed who had dreams of a life with her love? You can't do it, you just can't – you need to look at how the loss affects the person who is left behind, and you try to empathise with them. Recently I met an old man who was upset about local vandals. To him, it was ruining his life. He must have been over eighty years old, and he couldn't settle, couldn't find a moment's peace, because of the noise and the worry that it could start at any minute. For him, his life was wrecked. For him that sort of terror is real. My heart ached for what he was going through, but should I have said, 'Oh, I'm sorry, I can't listen to you or give you any sympathy, because my daughter died.'

But I can't be like that. I can't be cold when other people are hurting, and I can't understand for the life of me how others can do it.

I think the thing is, people know they will feel regret and remorse and guilt when they lose a child, or when someone they know suffers a loss like that, but they don't know what to do with the happiness. And there will be happiness, because life goes on. It's an odd thing to unpack. When you experience bereavement, *any* bereavement, there will be sympathy but that doesn't last forever: people who aren't in it with you only allow a certain amount of time before they expect you to be over it. They will say things like, 'Of course, it'll be hard, but she wouldn't want you to be sad forever' or that old classic 'Life goes on'. I *know* that! Of course I know all of that. When they meet you after six months, or a year or even five years, they want to see something has changed because they themselves don't know how to deal with it. Maybe that's because they're scared of grief – perhaps they've never lost someone, or maybe they're just emotionally unable to connect. They don't want you to cry, they don't want you to wail and say you feel as raw as you ever did. So, the burden lies with the bereaved – we're the ones who are expected to make the other person feel better, to look for a glimmer of hope, to start the conversation by saying, 'Ah, but the good news is . . .'

And then do you know what happens?

If we are *too* happy, or the news is *too* good, we're made to feel bad about that. New baby, new partner . . . well, hasn't she moved on? Sometimes I feel as if I can't win. People – not close family or close friends, but many other people – want me to be a particular type of Sara Payne. They want me to fit in with their expectations of what a grieving mother should be like, their timescale and their response, and, if I don't do that, they falter. I've always been my own person though, Sarah – I refuse to change for anyone else. I walk my own path and one of the things I really want to get over to others is that there is no wrong way to be when you have suffered the loss of a child. Be whatever you need to be, because it's *your* heart that's broken, it's *you* who has the empty bed in your home.

So, take happiness where you can find it. Laugh when you can. Sing when you can. You will feel enough guilt when you are doing those things and get a flash of what isn't there, so don't let other people make it worse. The thing is, we will all lose someone. Unless we have no human emotion at all, we will all hurt and we will all cry. So, why put in rules for the bereaved that we will soon know don't mean a thing?

When your child dies, part of you dies too. You want to crawl into the coffin beside them and hide forever. You don't want to feel; you really don't want to live. If I didn't have Lee and Luke and Charlotte back then, who knows what my life would have been? Who knows what might have happened? But then there would have been no Ellie – and that wouldn't have been right at all. What I know for certain is that you haven't really left me; you're beside me every moment of every day and the important part of us will never be separated. To hell with anyone who thinks I don't behave appropriately. They see laughter but they don't see how much it takes for me to get there; they see the public me but they don't know the barriers I still have around me; they see the confident campaigner but they don't see the broken heart that aches for you. None of that matters, not really – there are bigger things to be done, greater things to be achieved.

We're on the march now, Sarah. I feel all of my grief has finally made something wonderful, and that you are going to save so many children. xx

2007

John Reid isn't at the Home Office any more, and I miss him a great deal. He was such an honest man, there were no airs and graces about him, and I appreciated that he saw me for me. A woman called Jacqui Smith has taken his place and while she won't fill the gap completely, I'm finding her very easy to work with too. She's put me on lots of boards and made sure I have plenty of connections, Sarah. It's all coming together and I think she sees what needs to be done as well.

Jacqui was the one who saw that I was the only person in all of this who wasn't getting paid, so she's formalised my position and now I'm an official consultant. I have an official status now I guess, but it's come at a price. Not all of the children's charities are happy with me being given what they regard as an 'elevated status'. Some of them are questioning my place in all of this and there are constant digs that I'm only there as a *News of the World* mole, but that couldn't be further from the truth. It's me, Sarah, I'm the one who fought; I'm the one who wouldn't let this go, who knew there needed to be something done in your memory – I couldn't let it all be for nothing.

I find some of them absolutely impossible to work with but I'll keep at it, I'll keep fighting your corner for all of the children out there who are being failed by how things are at the moment. I get so frustrated – we cross swords too much and I can't see why they don't just concentrate on what they are there for. All they need to do is work for children, all they need to do is protect children, but they're so obsessed with their little power plays and their salaries and who has the ear of which minister, they forget those basic truths. Maybe that's arrogant of me. Maybe it's arrogant of me to think that I can tell what their job is, but I know that I wouldn't be able to sleep at night if I had the attitude of some of them. I guess it's unusual for them to have to deal with someone like me, an outsider coming in and being able to make such big changes, but we're both coming from the same place, I suppose – I need to try and remember that.

I think Jacqui likes my approach – she tells me about the policies, and I tell her what the real effect will be. We're a decent team, theory and practice. She says it's pretty unusual for someone to tell the Home Secretary where they're going wrong, but I've been lucky to work with two home secretaries who are willing to listen. I'm learning a lot from her too, but sadly much of it comes from the fact that there seems to be just one awful abuse case after another. There has been a terrible situation at a Jersey care home, Haut de la Garenne, where allegations of abuse over many, many years are being investigated. It worries me that the police don't use all the powers they have, but when I said to Jacqui that we needed to get to Jersey and see what was going on and sort things out, she told me it wasn't as simple as that. Although Jersey is under our laws, there are huge cultural differences and it just wouldn't be acceptable for the UK mainland government to arrive, with an attitude that they were going to fix everything. This is hard for me; it's hard to understand that there is a government point of view.

Although I'm there as the human face of policy, that just isn't enough in some cases. I think Jacqui, like so many other people, is surprised that I'm not an angry person. I'm always having to explain to people there would be no point – I don't want to tarnish your memory with anger or hatred, I'm just there to put the voice of the children across, to try and move things forward. I still believe that if you make a small change, you can bring about a big difference.

I could write a handbook on grief – or maybe not. It's different for everyone and for every relationship, I've said that before. To begin with, it's shock. You're in limbo, not feeling anything. There's no beating of the chest, no wailing. You mean to come back to the grief but you don't always have the time. Maybe that's a way of getting through; maybe if you lie to yourself, say you will revisit it, you can get away with the lie and be able to cope for a little longer. Life has to continue; it must go on hold until you get time, even if that time never comes. I had PTSD and so, actually, I could compartmentalise pretty well – I could put things in different boxes. It's all relative, grief, there are no rules, but PTSD actually worked for me sometimes. Society has expectations of what the bereaved are meant to do, but the truth is, you do what you need to do. Be selfish if you need to be. I wasn't because of the kids, but I wish I could have been. If you're supporting someone, let *them* be selfish. Let them talk or be quiet, or cry, or be alone, whatever they need. Above all, live for the person who has gone. You carry people in your heart forever and there's always a piece of them with you, their essence really, but I have seen too many people leave – this year, it was my dad. He had been ill for so long, and I'm not sure he ever got over what happened to you, princess, and he felt the loss of Nanny so much. He's still here, though; you all are. Not as ghosts or as angels, but as something that is with me, an aura of them maybe. I talk to my parents all the time – I know how they'd talk to me when I needed them. You need to acknowledge older people's knowledge, and I miss that, so I try to think of what they would say when I'm in trouble, when things are just a bit too dark. If I get days when I don't want to face the world, the kids do it for me, and I acknowledge my parents and that they would be telling me to do what I need to do. So I stay in bed, watch TV, have some alone time with my thoughts and memories. It's wrong to bury your children no matter the age but it's hard to bury your parents too.

Some people have tried to fix me but because of the scale and public interest, I'm unique so they don't know quite what to do with me. There's an element of 'you still going on?' when people meet me. There have been years of grieving and it won't stop, it won't ever stop, so the world just needs to get used to me being here and not giving up. Time doesn't matter and it doesn't heal, you just get used to the pain the way you would get used to losing a limb. Sadly, you also get used to life without that person.

Sometimes it's overwhelming and I do have to give in. There is such a black hole around me that wants to suck me in, given half the chance. I feel bereft, I do, but it's far too scary to allow myself to get sucked in and risk never coming out again.

Somehow, life is going on and your brothers and sisters are growing up even if you aren't. Bumping into your friends is hard when you're eight years old forever. I see them now and I get angry. The grief floods me and I feel robbed; but not on a day-to-day basis. Sometimes people offer the strangest things, psychic readings or conversations.

I've even had them offer to do portraits of how you'd look now. But I always refuse – I just have to look at my other kids to know, you're all so similar. You share so much.

And then it all happened again: another little girl, gone without a trace. It was in another country this time, but when Madeleine McCann disappeared in Praia da Luz, Portugal, on holiday with her parents in May 2007, the location didn't matter. But this time two things have been different, princess: Maddie has never been found, and her mum and dad have been treated horrifically.

People have judged them in the most awful way. Kate and Gerry McCann were having a meal in their villa while their daughter slept inside. When they went to check on her, she was gone. And for that, no one has forgiven them. We've all made decisions we've regretted, especially on holiday when we've been more relaxed. They weren't that far away, but for some reason the initial sympathy and concern of the public has turned to suspicion and something very close to hatred. I don't understand it.

The McCanns paid more than dearly – they lost their child and what can be worse than that? Only that child knows what truly happened and she still hasn't been found. For me the seventeen days were horrendous while you were missing, Sarah, so I don't know how they're coping. Hope is such a cruel thing but you need it to stay alive. You're frozen in the moment and that's what will be happening to Gerry and Kate now.

There has been a team of journalists working on the story that I know and I was asked to do TV very quickly, to talk about being in that position, but as with other cases, I will only ever do that if the parents ask me. I'd do it then. As soon as a child goes missing, my phone is red hot, but I know that I'm associated with the worst outcome. I was so horrified by how the McCanns have been getting treated and I wouldn't add to that for the world. I think the way people have taken a dislike to them all boils down to the first view. People judged Kate on how she first reacted and that's wrong; she was a rabbit stuck in headlights and she was the one that bore the brunt – the mother, the woman. My heart went out to her and when people went after them, I was so upset. I felt sick that they were judged as if they deserved it. The balance tore me in two – how could I help without making it worse? You have to think in these cases – what if the missing child is watching? All the child needs to hear is 'We're coming to find you'. People are easily distracted, they forget; when they went after Kate and Gerry McCann, they seemed to forget how supportive they had been of me. And there's the apathy – they scapegoat the mother rather than ask the hard questions. It all needs to be offloaded – let the courts decide who is guilty in a case like this, not people who get emotional and only look at one aspect.

You get thrown into it when you've lost a child, there's no preparation but all of a sudden the world is watching. I remember not wanting the front door closed in case you came back – I didn't want you to think that I wasn't waiting for you. But how long can you sustain that level of hope before it destroys you? There's a piece of me that will always look for you, Sarah, and I bet the McCanns will always look for Maddie. I have so many dreams where you just walk back in and it has all been a big mistake. I'd have you back tomorrow but we'd have such different lives and I know that it would be for me, not for you, because you would be broken.

We had the police working with us from the start. That was a big help. Poor Kate. It must have been crazy when it began, and it hasn't got any better. When the news first broke, I was sitting watching TV, thinking, *at least get her an interpreter.* Imagine being in a foreign country, listening to a language you don't understand, and your child has gone missing, just disappeared. Half of the time she wouldn't even know what was being said – more than half the time – so when she wasn't reacting in a way people wanted, how did they even know she knew what was going on? Society wants someone to blame and there was no identified child snatcher, so they turned on her: they turned on the woman. It's because mothers are expected to be a certain thing, to act in a certain way, and Kate wasn't what was wanted: she was a doctor, she was educated, she was seen as something apart – but she was just a lost parent, wanting to hold her child again. She has been ripped to shreds, more than Gerry, and it's so unfair. She doesn't have time to be the right thing for everyone and that's disgusting.

Some people have no empathy: there's no forgiveness in the heart of some and it's a waste of time trying to convince them that the McCanns need support, support like we got. People dislike that they got a media expert in, but why wouldn't they, in a strange country, with so many things happening? There are very few cases like ours, like us and the McCanns, there is no rule book and I say do what you need to do. Kate McCann didn't seem the same as me, so people reacted against her, but I can't explain the level of shock you feel when you're in that zombie land. It has been such a mess, and the efforts should have gone into looking for Madeleine instead of criticising Kate and Gerry – smoke and mirrors, looking in the wrong place, hating the wrong people. The level of support for them has been so different. Everyone in the country was looking for you, Sarah, but that hasn't happened in Portugal and it seems there hasn't been one iota of empathy.

But this year . . . this year, Sarah … As if there hasn't been enough.

I had such headaches.

They were normal to start with, then – the pain, the pain. I got to the stage where I couldn't even move my head. After giving a talk to the Stroke Society in London in the early summer, I had a migraine for two whole weeks.

'This isn't normal,' Mole insisted, 'you need to get to the GP.'

'It's fine,' I assured him. 'I'm tough as old boots, it'll pass.'

'When? When will it pass?' he said. 'You're knocking back Nurofen by the box and just hoping it'll go, but it isn't going, Sara – it's getting worse.'

'It's fine,' I repeated. 'It *will* pass.'

But it didn't pass.

I got a bit of a sore throat, and combined with the migraine, finally had to admit defeat and take to my bed. I'd been getting nothing done and for me it was frustrating that this rotten headache was stopping me from getting on with things. When it came to the weekend, I'd decided.

'I've had enough of this,' I told Mole.

'Are you going to the GP at last?' he asked.

'No, I'm not going to let it get me down – let's go out for lunch,' I told him, defiantly.

I got dressed but the pain was awful – I felt as if my head was going to explode. By the time we arrived at the pub for lunch, I was in agony. I stumbled out of the car, weakly, and muttered to Mole, 'There's something wrong.'

'Shall we get you to the GP?' he asked.

'I think it's gone beyond that,' I said, finally admitting defeat as the pain shot through my head. 'I think we need to go to A&E.'

I was staggering around as if I was drunk, slurring and confused. By this point I'd been in pain for over a fortnight, but it had reached crisis point. Mole got me back in the car and drove to the nearest hospital. We were asked to wait for hours – they kept giving me painkillers, but that wasn't helping at all. So I sat there, holding the top of my head, as I felt it was about to blow off with the pressure.

Finally, I was sent for a CT scan. The hospital I was in didn't spot anything that concerned them, but the scans were automatically sent on to all the other hospitals in the region. Not long after they had told me that there was nothing to worry about, it was 'just' a headache and all my tests for conditions such as meningitis were negative, they received a call from one of those other places: something had been picked up. They had noticed a small bleed and wanted some further investigations. Within minutes I was being taken to St George's Hospital in Tooting, South London, blues and twos flashing. Worried beyond belief, Mole followed behind in his car.

I was taken straight to the Intensive Care Unit and . . . well, I don't really remember much of the two days following that. I do know that there was a nurse at the end of my bed the whole time and there were an awful lot of worried faces. After those two days, a decision was made – I needed an operation, and I needed it immediately. The doctors didn't know how much damage was still being done inside my brain as the bleed was ongoing. Everyone was in shock.

As soon as the doctor shook Luke's hand, your brother ran from the room. I could see the terror on his face. *What now?* he seemed to be thinking.

He wasn't the only one with questions.

I could see Mole waiting, thinking, plucking up the courage to ask what he really wanted to know.

'What if she doesn't have the op?' he asked.

The doctor looked at him. 'That isn't an option, I'm afraid.'

It's so strange to hear things like that when you're only listening, when you aren't part of the conversation. *Not an option*. So, I had to take this risk, I had to have the operation. The doctors explained to Mole that they had no idea what was going on, that there was still a bleed in my brain, and if they didn't stop it, the damage could be lethal. They didn't know how much of my brain had already been affected, but they knew they had to get in there and stop it or there would be no going back.

The ICU was so quiet and relaxed, but that changed once I started to get prepped for the operation. There were more people and there was an air of efficiency that felt different to the morphine fog I'd been in. I'd really just been sleeping a lot, and I was still very dopey, but I knew something major was taking place. The doctors wanted to clip the bleed under anaesthetic, but the thing that worried me was much more superficial. As the anaesthetist started to take me down to theatre, all I could think was that they were going to cut my beautiful, long brown hair.

'Please don't,' I begged, 'please don't cut my hair.'

'There are more important things than that,' he replied.

Not to me, I thought.

I don't remember anything else really until I woke up

many hours later in the recovery room, and the first person I saw was Lee.

Actually, no – I need to go back a bit, don't I, princess? That wasn't the first thing I remember. There was something before and I think you'll know what I mean. As I was coming round from the anaesthetic, I felt as if I had a choice: I didn't have to reach consciousness if I didn't want to. It sounds dramatic, but it was actually very gentle. There was a voice in my head – was it you, Sarah? – telling me that I could choose, that it was up to me. I then heard Lee, Luke, Charlotte and Ellie all calling me, pulling me back to them. Was it real? Was it a dream? I think I know, I think you do too. I had to choose, darling, didn't I? I had to choose who to be with.

I'm so tired, Sarah – not just with everything that has happened this year, but everything that has happened with *all* the years. Do you have any idea how tempting it was to just give up? It was so lovely to see you and there was a part of me that wanted to say, *yes, it's time to stop, it's time to be with you*. I would like that very much indeed, for us to be together, and for the fight to be over – but then, when I heard their voices, I knew I had to stay for them all because I don't think they could cope without me: they need me more than you do, Sarah. When I did decide, when I decided to stay with them, I started to come round. It was wonderful to see Mole's face but the sheer terror and concern in his eyes made me realise I had done the right thing. I still have to be strong for them, I still have to be what they need me to be, and you'll just have to wait a little while longer, my love.

The first thing I said to them all was, 'Let's get up and get this sorted.' However, it wasn't quite so easy as that. I still had a terrible headache, for one thing. For a while I didn't see my scar as I wasn't mobile and I didn't have access to a mirror, so it was quite a shock when I finally did. It was absolutely huge with seven staples on the outside – for me, the worst thing of all was that my head was almost shaved. It might sound silly that I was so concerned about my hair but I think I was just focusing on that one thing to avoid thinking about how awful everything else had been. My hair had always been such a huge part of my identity and now it was gone. I knew it would grow back again, but it was a symbol of how much I'd gone through.

I stayed in hospital for a couple of weeks and was on such a high when I left. It seemed a sign that I had survived something like such a severe aneurysm at such a young age. Not many people go through that at forty-two, and I feel it was because I still have so much more to give. I'm so lucky to be alive, Sarah, and to be pretty much unaffected. I feel as if I can take on the world again. True, close encounters with death don't leave you unscathed, but I didn't really have any physical after-effects at all. I was just suffering from dehydration a bit, and there were continuing headaches – I guess I appeared a little tipsy at times, to be honest!

'There's been enough messing around,' I told Mole, 'let's get on with this. I've chosen life for a reason.'

It's still a bit of a shock to me that I had done that. I'd wanted to be with you for so long but then, when I had that opportunity, I didn't take it. For years I've been feeling guilty that I'm here and you're not, and I still do because I'm full of this amazing energy and there's even more guilt for not following the path that would have taken me to your side forever. I guess it's just not in me to give up. I'd been exhausted and I could have gone, but how could I leave? Have they not been through enough? I'd have been giving him my life and I've always promised never to do that. Roy Whiting didn't really get you because you are still in the hearts and minds of everyone, and he will never get me.

Let's go, Sarah — let's go again. xx

2008

MY DARLING GIRL —

Last year, when I put my heels on and walked out of hospital, thinking everything was great, I had absolutely no idea how serious it all was and how much my life was going to change yet again. The problem has been that I've kept having headaches. Ellie is a really noisy child, so it's hard to have that around me all the time; she's never quiet. My head hurts a lot and I worry with each headache. I probably overanalyse things but I have to say to everyone that I'm fine. I do believe that it's time to start living and get back on with campaigning, but the headaches worry me, if I'm truthful.

I'm so sorry that I'm not with you, darling. I don't mean that I want to die, I just want to be with you — that's different. If I had died, if I had given up when I saw you, I would be with you, you know. Sometimes I want that so badly. I'm torn, there's a constant battle in my head – I want to be with you, I want to be with the others. I want to live, but I know I have to die if we're to be together again. Little Ellie is still so small – despite the noise she makes! – and she needs me, they all do. I feel such a bad person for even making the choice though; it's not one I could ever feel comfortable with because you were pitted against them.

I do feel positive, because being alive is such a privilege, but I miss you so badly and I feel that was my one chance to be with you. I need to live for you, don't I? I don't have the right to waste this life as it's one you don't have. I think we all feel that now, at last. We need to stop wishing our lives away, but we've needed the shock of my aneurysm to get that huge turnaround in emotions.

So, I'll go on. I'll go on wearing my two hats. I'll be Mum at home and Sara who works on all the hard stuff when I go out. I'm trying to make weekends a real family focus – I don't bring work home and I spend all my time from Friday night until Monday morning just with the kids. It's a sad fact that Dad isn't doing well at all. He's drinking so much, bingeing a lot, and I need to be the calm one for your brothers and sisters. I need them to keep their distance when he's in that mode as I don't want them being damaged by it. I don't know what the future will hold for your dad, I really don't, but he seems to be on such a destructive path. The aneurysm was such a shock, even more so when the doctors told me that not many survive, so I do feel, more than ever, that there is a purpose for me, and I can't let worry about your dad get in the way of that.

Someone asked Mole about what happened, and how I had got through it when so many don't, and he said, 'Nothing stops her – she's an absolute steamroller; she has this knack of moving forward, no matter what.' I guess he's right – I believe everyone needs to just develop that knack of moving forward, no matter what. Dust yourself off and hold your head high, get on with whatever it is. I've taken my own advice; I bounced back and I have to say, apart from the headaches, I feel fine. There doesn't seem to be any residual effects and I've been able to carry on working, working in your name.

When the headaches come, I try to rest for a few days and ignore them as best I can, because I really can't allow myself to dwell on things. I've learned to keep myself hydrated as that can keep the headaches at bay sometimes, but, other than that, life continues. I'm actually full of energy most of the time, now that I have decided to grab every moment. I'm going at everything full throttle – no matter what it is, it gets my full attention. There will be no more putting my head in the sand and I certainly won't allow grief to slow me down. If I have unhappy thoughts, I try to look beyond them and find a happy memory.

★

I'd been a fool. I hadn't considered that my body was giving me a serious warning. Maybe looking back, I should have listened. I was completely fooling myself that I could do everything – and something had to give.

Earlier this year, it was also announced that they would start rolling out your law in certain areas of the country to see how it would work, and what the response would be. I was elated at that – finally, the real stuff was happening. I started working at the Home Office, often sitting on the boards that would create Sarah's Law or the Child Sex Offender (CSO) Disclosure Scheme. I felt as if I had to prove myself to everyone there – they were the professionals and I was just an add-on. There had been quite a lot of criticism about the research I'd been doing, with some so-called professionals saying I was naïve, that I didn't see the bigger picture. I found this incredibly ironic as those were exactly the things I would say about them!

Every time someone claimed those things, I knew what they meant. If they said I was naïve, it meant they thought I was focusing too much on the victims and believing too much in the British public. If they said I was unable to see the bigger picture, I knew it meant they were pretty short-sighted themselves and would be the ones who were called for the rights of perpetrators, rolling out sob stories about how badly they were treated and how they'd all had awful upbringings. It was an insult, Sarah. They are plenty of good, upstanding, caring and loving people who have the most hideous of childhoods, but they make the choice to break free of that. Do these professionals truly believe that every abused child becomes an abuser? Given how much I now know about how many children experience abuse, I can tell them one thing straight away – they couldn't cope with what would happen if every abused child went down that route as an adult. Society would fall apart. It is a horrible thing to allege – to say to people who have done all they can to survive that they are one of *them*; that they are no better than the hideous creature who exposed them to such hell.

Another irony is that, as I've said on so many occasions, we don't believe the children who tell most of the time anyway. So, who is the priority here? When they say that I'm naïve, that I don't see the whole picture, I suspect that they just don't like someone coming from the outside and showing up the horrific gaps in a system that should, to my mind, have victims at the forefront of every single decision that is made.

I feel I can never talk about you to them, darling. I have to be professional, otherwise they would be all too quick to dismiss me as just some over-emotional grieving mother. Someone who was so blinded by grief that she couldn't see what was best for the world, that she couldn't stay in her box, that she couldn't just leave the big guns to deal with all the tricky things. Well, this over-emotional grieving mother won't stand for that. I will take their cues, and I will box away all I feel about you, and I will fight. It makes me a bit bombastic at times, but they'll just have to deal with that. I'm like a dog with a stick – I won't give up and I won't stop.

I know that everyone thinks I'm so confident, but it's all a front, really. It's not that I think I know better, it's that I'm willing to learn, and they are sometimes just so stubborn. It's as if they are the experts, they know it all, and they can't imagine that an ordinary person who has spoken to other ordinary people could teach them anything. I have the opposite approach: I'm always willing to learn. I never once thought that I knew better than them, I really didn't, so I absorbed as much knowledge as I could from everyone and anyone in the meetings. I would listen to everything then turn their arguments into an answer. All I did was apply common sense and my own real-life experience of just being a mum at the school gates. I took as much of real life as possible to the meetings, as much as I possibly could.

And then, Sarah, the most wonderful news: I found out I was to be this year's Special Award winner at the Children's Champion awards gala from the *News of the World*. I had attended as a guest several times and I knew all of the team, but this time, it was so different because I got the award!

I felt like an A-list celebrity. I wasn't really comfortable with it but tried really hard to play the part. It was so lovely, an absolute dream evening for me for once. I was a girly girl! You would have loved it, all the sparkles and shine – I think you were there with me, weren't you? I think you were encouraging me, saying that this was a good thing because it made sure the issue was in people's minds. When they saw me, they remembered, and that was important. Mole was at my side the whole time, looking so dashing in his dinner suit. He rarely watches TV so didn't really know who anyone was, but he still knew it was a special night. The journalists were all so good – they knew that we didn't want to go public on our relationship, so they cut him out of the pictures. Some of them passed on copies of the two of us privately for me to keep, but they never splashed it all over the front pages, and I was very grateful for that. Mole smiled the whole evening, full of pride, and, for once, I felt that way too, even if it came at a cost. I was there for a reason; I was there because I didn't have you.

There is so much going on, and I barely have time to catch my breath. I feel as if I dodged a bullet with my health last year, but as this year goes on, I've started to feel quite poorly again. I don't know what's ahead of me, Sarah, I'll just take it as it comes.

In February, Levi Bellfield was found guilty of the murder of thirteen-year-old schoolgirl Milly Dowler. I think the same of him as I think of the creature that took you. These men don't deserve our attention, they get too much of it. They shouldn't be allowed near good and decent people ever again. Bellfield was from the area where we used to live, and I recognised his name while the case was going on. I wasn't close to him, but your dad knew him and they'd had a drink together in the past.

It never seems to end, Sarah. Another little girl has been taken too, a nine-year-old called Shannon Matthews, who is missing from West Yorkshire. Her poor family is distraught and her mum, Karen, has been on the news, begging for the return of her daughter. There are so many reports from the police and media about Shannon and it's hitting too close to home.

Sometimes I think that we've got past all of this, you know. Maybe it's because of what happened last year, but sometimes I see us, in my mind, and we're walking. It's a beautiful day, the sun is shining, and it's just us. You're eight years old, as you always are, but you're so wise. You say to me that you never wanted to put me through all of this, you never wanted to put any of us through it.

I tell you, *it wasn't your fault!* I never want you to think any of it was ever your fault – how could it be?

You hold my hand and say that you have missed us all, but we've got through it now – and I wonder, will that ever happen? Will I feel we have ever got through it?

When I have those daydreams, when I think that one day you and I will look back on it all, I can almost believe it. Are they a prediction of the future? Will that happen? I don't believe in anything particularly woo, but I need something to hold onto. When I see that poor woman, Shannon's mum, on TV, I know what she's going through. Kate McCann is going through the same, and Milly

Dowler's family will have to make their way through life now, knowing what was done to their beautiful girl. So, I'm waiting – I'm waiting for the next announcement. Of course we all still have to have hope that Shannon is found, safe and well, but there will always be another Shannon. Another Milly. Another Maddie.

Another you.

And that is the part of the world that I hate.

They have found Shannon – but, princess, such an awful story. She is alive and safe now but it should never have happened in the first place. Her own mother was behind it all, Sarah, how awful is that?

That poor child was found in the home of a man who was the uncle of her mum's boyfriend. Almost a month after she went missing, Shannon was found, hidden in the base of a bed, kidnapped for the attention and the money her mother thought people would donate to an appeal.

I can barely get my head round it.

What a wicked woman – how dare she take the kindness of the country and do this? It is all so twisted, when the backstory of Shannon's life has been told; you have to wonder what did she go through every day with a mother like that? Why wasn't Karen Matthews stopped? In some situations there should be interference, someone should step in. Why have kids if you have no interest in them? As the story is coming out, it looks as if she was drawn in by the disappearance of little Madeleine McCann. She

saw the attention and she saw that people were giving
money to the fund that was trying to find her, and she
wanted some of that. It beggars belief. The worst thing in
the world is when your child disappears, and I can't even
begin to comprehend how a mother could choose to do
that to her own daughter. To come up with a plan to do
a fake kidnapping and then to actually allow that child
to think it was all happening to her – that is horrific. For
almost a month, Shannon must have believed it was true;
that her life was in danger, she had been taken from her
family. And now? How can that poor child ever recover
from knowing her own mother was behind it? From
knowing that the one person who should have kept her
safe and sound forever was part of this monstrous plan
to kidnap her own child for money and some TV news
conferences? She may not really have been kidnapped
by a Roy Whiting or a Levi Bellfield, but will she ever
recover from being betrayed by the woman who gave
birth to her?

It's beyond me why anyone would seek that sort of
attention. When I think of what we have lost to get to that
stage – there is nothing, nothing worth losing a child for.
When I think of how Karen Matthews smirked her way
through news conferences and of how I thought I'd never
manage. When I think of how she said the things I said
to you, knowing that you were safe, knowing that *she* had
done it . . . I feel sick.

★

It's finally happened, princess — Sarah's Law trials started this September for six months. Parents in the test areas can ask the police if they are worried about someone involved in their child's life, whether it's a new partner or a neighbour. The test areas are Peterborough in Cambridgeshire, Stockton in Cleveland, Southampton and all of Warwickshire, and parents there can check on the background of anyone who can be close to their child that they are unsure of. The mum or dad has to prove their identity to the police and then fill in a form saying what they're worried about. Following this the police will carry out an immediate check on the individual, taking no more than twenty-four hours. If the child is in danger, the police have to act immediately. Then they have to carry out a full risk assessment involving other child protection agencies and social services. The checks shouldn't take any longer than six weeks. I'm so excited that it's finally going live, my darling.

The next step is for the police and MAPPA (Multi-Agency Public Protection Arrangements) teams, which supervise convicted sex offenders, to discuss what they have found out and whether it will be passed on. If they find out the person is a convicted paedophile, there is a 'presumption' that information that is 'relevant, necessary and proportionate' will be given to parents. Parents may also be told if police have intelligence about the person or details of convictions which are non-sexual but may also put the child at risk, such as a history of domestic abuse.

Parents can't tell other people what they find out. What the police tell parents must be kept confidential. If the police fear parents will tell others they can decide not to reveal the information. There are civil punishments for passing on the information and criminal penalties if it is used to provoke an attack on the paedophile. It's not perfect, but it's a start and we have to be careful.

It's different from the US, where much more information is available, and without you having to ask for it. Many states use Megan's Law to put names, addresses, photographs and details of convictions on websites. There were fears such a law would prompt paedophiles to evade the authorities, making them more difficult to monitor and it might also breach human rights laws – always looking out for the perpetrator, but finally doing something, even if it isn't quite enough.

Sometimes there is such happiness, Sarah, such good news! I have just discovered that I am to be given an MBE. The New Year's Honours List will be out in a few days and it will be announced then. I am such a Royalist, but you know that – this is a huge honour. I'm excited and nervous, and, actually, I feel a little bit undeserving. It matters because it keeps the issue in the public eye, but I've only done what needed to be done. I know that's a problem I have, that I underestimate what has been achieved, but I haven't done it alone – you've been with me on the whole journey.

All the attention and the good feelings that come with

this sort of thing . . . well, I feel a bit of a fraud, if truth be told. There is a massive team behind me, behind *us*: Team Sara, Team Sarah. Our family, the guys at the paper, the other journalists who have helped, people like John Reid … so many of them. I feel one day, someone will find out that I'm just winging it.

Sometimes, it's as if I've been put on a pedestal. The truth is, I just grabbed every opportunity with both hands. I absorbed everyone else's knowledge and learning, even if it was something I knew nothing of. I will be so proud of this MBE, Sarah. I will never feel worthy of such a high accolade, but I will always attempt to live up to the standard set by our beloved monarchy, and the values instilled in me by my parents. They would have been over the moon and it's their love and the way they taught me that decent, hard-working people can achieve so much that has brought me to this point. They made me believe that you should always make the best of all and any situation, that life is never as dark as you might think. Well, my love, we faced that darkness and it was pretty bloody dark, but there is light – there is always light.

If you look, if you can find the courage to hope, there will always be something to cling onto. And I had my family; maybe there was one person missing but I still had the others, and as time has gone on, the worry that I had when I used to talk and write to you has actually become a comfort. I thought, at first, that it was a sign I might go mad. It has actually kept me sane; it has kept you close to me.

I love the noise and the madness of a family; I hate the quiet and don't want to get used to it. I love school holidays, the long days and nights. If I can keep busy, I can keep the quiet away. I can make an endless summer. Do you know there are people who think I made millions from losing you? That I wanted to become some sort of twisted celebrity? How cruel is that? They don't understand that the child – whatever child, whether mine or not – is the important thing for me. By keeping in touch with you, princess, I have tried to keep you in this world, keep you making some noise in my life, I guess.

Has it worked? I think it has – I really think it has. We should be proud of what we have achieved together, my darling. You are making the world a safer place. xx

2009

We have needed this event to look forward to – the MBE ceremony! You know that I worry about the others, especially your brothers and Charlotte, the ones who were there with you. How angry are they going to be at the world? They certainly do have some anger even now, but it's mostly sadness. We rarely speak of that day but I know that they do amongst themselves. It's a work in progress, there's no ending here, but something like this wonderful event gives us all hope.

It was such a good day, sweetheart, but I was so sad that my parents weren't there to see it – they'd have been very, very proud. On 7 April Luke and Charlotte and Mole and I went to Windsor Castle for the ceremony. I wore a floral summer dress and the Queen was so kind. Imagine that, I can say she was kind because she spoke to me! She asked me how I was coping and said that she had followed your story, my love. I told her about the ongoing work with the government but, of course, she knew all about it. She said it was a terrible thing but I don't really know how much she knew – maybe she was told what to say.

'How are you? Does working help?' she asked me.

'Being busy stops me dwelling on things,' I replied. And I think a look passed between us that made me feel she knew exactly what I meant.

I curtsied, and there were a lot of pleasantries, but it was all a bit of a blur as it was so wonderful. I feel odd telling you all of this because you're with me all the time, we've done this together – you're always at my side, aren't you?

The Queen spent exactly the same amount of time with everyone – Mole timed it. What she did was perfect, I know that.

Work goes on – it can't be a visit to a castle to meet the Queen every day! I've got a new job now. Justice Secretary Jack Straw has created a role for me as the Victims' Champion. Personally I think it's a terribly naff title, but it's the thought that counts. I suppose it's the best way to describe the job. My post is for a year and it's to set everything up so that they can hit the ground running when the Commissioner's job is established – I think they want me to take on that role but who knows what will happen?

I had been in talks about this role quite a lot when Jacqui Smith was home secretary and always asked when they were going to put a Victims' Commissioner in place; there needs to be more in place first, I was told, and I guess this is it. I had hoped I would be asked to interview for the role as I felt I could really make the necessary changes and do a good job.

I was asked to go in and see Jack Straw in, I think, November, which was perfect for me – I had a couple of things I wanted to raise with him about some of the cases I was advocating for, and I needed his attention and support.

I went to London to meet with him and I was told that I could interview for the job at the same time. Everything was just as it had been with all my other visits – chatting to staff, seeing people I knew – until I was asked to go in to see Jack Straw himself. When I entered the room, I was faced with a panel of people: representatives from government, charities, and the Civil Service. They asked so many questions but all I could really do was be myself. So I answered quite calmly, chatting away, and it didn't really feel like an interview at all. One thing they did focus on was my relationship with the press – how did I feel that would work if I was an insider? I answered honestly, as I always do. If the public needed to know something, I would tell them. I would be happy to use my contacts but I wouldn't do things that would come as a surprise to my employers – I would tell Jack Straw beforehand and he would have a chance to put his side across. I'm not a devious person and I felt that, actually, the public needed to know an awful lot more about the justice system than they did. It was true that I would bring press attention to the role, but that was something that could be seen in a positive light. They needed to remember that if it hadn't been for the press attention I had received in the first place, you, Sarah, might be nothing more than a statistic. I wasn't willing to work in secrecy or in private – as long as we all understood that, things would be fine.

I think the reason they gave me the job was because they liked my honesty. They were also relieved – although maybe a little sceptical – that my ties to the press were entirely voluntary on both sides. I didn't have a contract with anyone, just verbal agreements that had never been broken. When they did offer me the job, I was sworn to secrecy until it was officially announced. Maybe that was a test in itself, but it didn't bother me and I didn't even tell Shy [Keenan] in advance. She was so proud and we both agreed that I could do a huge amount at government level, which meant I should really take a year-long sabbatical from Phoenix [see Appendix, p.000] so that no lines were crossed. So, that's what I did.

I've still been talking to Shy, as she's at the coalface really. I need to discuss with her how things will translate in real life and she's my best friend, so she knows how I work. I keep up to date on any cases I worked on before I took my sabbatical, just because it's important to me that I take as many voices with me as I can. These things can't just be from my perspective. I'm well aware that my experience of the justice system is not the same as most: I was treated very well and I've always said that if it can be done once then it can be done across the board. All victims of all crimes should be dealt with in the same way that my family had been – with respect, understanding and empathy. It's not too much to ask.

Every story I've heard I carry with me and it informs all of the work I do. Every victim and every victim's family I've spoken to stays in my heart. Those are the people I'm loyal to, the ones I try to change the world for. There is just so much injustice, Sarah – when someone is murdered, their family then has to stand by as their character is assassinated, and there's no one to defend them. I've looked all over for the answers – to other countries, to other systems – but I can't see that anywhere truly keeps the needs of the victim and their family at the centre of what they do.

We need to take bits from lots of systems. Ours is antiquated. We don't need to stick with history, we can move forward without disrespecting it. I'm a Royalist and a Parliamentarian but I want things to change when they have to. Sometimes I think I should stand as an MP but they work so hard, I'm not sure I would have that energy or mental capacity.

I'm not a one-horse pony but the Department of Justice is where I feel at home – that's where I was meant to be in life, I think. It's where I can make the most difference. John Reid's legacy lives on – he split the Justice and

Home Office departments overnight, really. The civil servants were furious but the political landscape was too big for each department, they needed change. I liked John very much as you know, and I miss that he isn't there with me now. He always said, 'You got through the door because of Murdoch but you're the reason you stayed.' I was flattered by those words then and they stay in my mind to this day. For a long time, I rode on the *News of the World* name in the minds of many people, but John challenged that and his words gave me a lot of confidence that I am still utilising.

When someone these days is a bit snobby with me, or treats me as if I'm just some daft mum who is out of her depth, I always think of the first time he called me, directly on my mobile phone.

'Hello, it's John Reid,' he said, with no preamble from an assistant.

I was a bit confused. 'Who?' I asked, used to having to jump through hoops to speak to the powers that be.

'Home Secretary,' he laughed.

I was embarrassed not to recognise him, but I did have a million things on my mind. 'Yes, Mr Reid – what can I do for you?'

'Well, you can call me John for a start,' he said.

He was lovely to me – straight-talking, no airs and graces – but I can't say everyone is the same. I try and fix him in my mind's eye at difficult times, wishing he hadn't gone on to other things as we could have done so much more together. He took me very, very seriously but some of the new team don't. From the moment he asked me to go and see him and tell him what I'd uncovered, I knew we could work together as a team, right from the off. It was easy – I was the eyes and ears on the ground. When he retired, I was at his leaving do, the only civilian there, and I appreciated that gesture. He had such sparkly eyes, such an honest little Scottish man with a hint of devilment about him – we need more like him, Sarah.

I do have to address my own prejudices and see politicians as people, I've always recognised that. I know they are constrained because I see the inner workings of government and it isn't as straightforward as some people might imagine. It was the former Shadow Home Secretary Ann Widdecombe who said that Sarah's Law would never happen but I knew it would because it was the right thing and they needed to listen to the British public. There's more than just PR to politics but it's an awful lot for me to balance – there's always a network behind every working woman and I need it more than most.

People still talk about you, Sarah; they don't avoid it. The media have always taken a shine to me and they are still on my side. The PTSD continues to help me compartmentalise – one hat on, then another, whichever hat is best for the situation I'm in. As soon as I walk in the door, I can't be *that* Sara Payne at home. I promise myself I will always be Mum first. Ellie has never known me any other way. She does long hours at school, with breakfast and after-school clubs. Always fiercely independent, she doesn't really rely on me much at all. She is looking more and more like you, darling – on her first day at school, the teacher gasped. 'It's not Sarah,' I explained. 'They're very different.'

Ellie will argue black is white. Because all of her siblings are much older, she doesn't see adults in the same way you did: she sees herself on their level. It's always been a flat playing field for her. She sees me taking on the world and I think that's made her who she is. Mole always says I am a superhero and she believes that. I don't let Ellie watch the news really so she can't understand why I'm famous but she knows the other mums aren't the same.

My work with the government has a year's tenure. I've been travelling the length and breadth of the country seeing the justice system from the official view then looking at it from the other side. They want me to impart the victim's side to them and vice versa, and I'm working on a document called 'Redefining Justice'. There are small things that can be done to make things better and I'm hoping these will be taken on and then I can fight for the big stuff. It's like doing a doctorate, really.

The PTSD sometimes rages, it's sometimes calm. I've had to learn to live with it. I breathe through it, but it's hard when the adrenalin is pumping. I've learned to hide it very well. Breathing deeply and drinking lots of water, that's the key. I've never allowed it to stop me doing anything, though.

I get flashes of you or the court case or the investigation. I can be in a room with people but I see them as a film in my head. When I'm out I fiddle with my hair to settle myself but then I come home and I'm completely grounded by what meets me – laundry all over the floor, dinner to be cooked, homework to be supervised. In the early hours, I catch up on housework or chat to friends or just sit in silence on my own. I try not to think about what has brought me to this place. My background does make me feel inferior – everyone I work with has been to a good school, they have degrees, privileged backgrounds, and it always makes me ask: am I as competent? It's a class thing, I know, and I need to move past it.

The adults I meet who were victims as children are the focus for me. Children do tell, but we don't listen. If they don't tell in words, they tell in actions, but we can't bear to pay attention. Look at how we react when there is something between a teenager and a teacher. We laugh and often say it's an affair. No, it's abuse – it's *always* abuse. They'll get called young adults, anything rather than the child they are. Why do we ignore them? No one likes to talk of sex crimes but we have to get past that. Some are so completely groomed that they use the language of their abuser and we need to recognise when that happens too.

I'm going to concentrate on the idea of Anti-Victim Prejudice when I finish my year on this job – the ideas are percolating with Shy. Really, we need to ask why would anyone tell they were abused when they get treated so badly? When they get described in such awful ways? In no other crime do you have to prove that you're not lying. Rape victims are treated atrociously from the start. Everyone I've spoken to has said they'd never encourage anyone to report and that worries me; it should worry the government too.

What drives me and Shy is what we can do for victims – and when other people recognise our work, it's such a boost. I don't mean that in a vain way, I just mean that it can feel thankless when so many people are against the change, so to get any little piece of recognition gives us some energy. I've just found out that, together, we've been given a Women of the Year Award and that means a great deal. Every time something like that happens, it brings publicity. Every time there is publicity, people will remember your case. Every time they remember your case, they ask what I'm doing now. Every time they ask what I'm doing now, I tell them. That's how it has to be: never stop, spread the message.

It's hitting home that Ellie finds life hard. No one in the family says things will be fine any more, they know differently: it is a difficult time. There is so much going on, and I really need a break. I feel as if something needs to give, but there is so much to do, so very much to do. xx

2010

SARAH, SWEET SARAH —

It's been a while since I have written, and I'm sorry that last year ended so abruptly. I have a reason though, babe. Just before Christmas, I was in London with my sister Fiona. She had a hospital appointment for her lupus and has to get lots of blood tests; it's routine for her but takes all day, so it's nice to give her a bit of company. All day, I had the most terrible headache. There was so much waiting around, and my head felt as if it was going to explode. Every time I get a headache now, I do feel a little worried after what happened last time with the aneurysm, but I try not to make anything of it, I try to remember that everyone gets headaches. This one just wouldn't go. By the time I got home, my head was splitting. I had so much to do – decorate the tree, get presents organised – and then, nothing.

That was it. I got home, I remember making a mental list of what I had to do, then . . . nothing.

I'd had a stroke, Sarah.

And it's only thanks to Mole that I'm still here today. He recognised the signs, knew I needed immediate attention, and called for an ambulance, telling them all of the symptoms. His quick thinking saved my life. I'd only gone to have a lie down, but when he checked on me, he saw that my face had dropped and I couldn't speak, so he called 999 and they rushed me in. I was taken to St Peter's Hospital in Chertsey – I had a scan, they did what was needed, and decided I had to get quick action due to my previous bleed. I was then rushed to St George's in Tooting – I had another stroke on top of that one in the ICU. Our family was told to go home and leave me to it.

So, I had two brain operations in thirty-six hours. Mole and the kids were told I had a fifty-fifty chance of survival, and would need further surgery after complications. I was in intensive care on a ventilator for two weeks.

When I had the stroke I thought I would see you again, sweetheart. I was paralysed down the left side but I chose to live. There have been times when being with you is all I want and, after the last time, when I did see you, it was so tempting to just go this time, to make that choice. When I had the previous aneurysm and was put to sleep for the clip to stop the bleeding, I thought, *well, if I don't wake up, it's my time; if I do, it's not.* I needed to get on with things and I needed to stay for the others and that made my decision for me; I wasn't physically saying 'no' back then, but I was so tired this time that maybe I wouldn't have had the strength.

However, there was no big white light, there was nothing dramatic. I've just been fighting ever since it happened. Your little nephew Alfie was born a few days after it happened, and I hate that I wasn't the grandmother I needed to be for him at the beginning. When faced with the choice, I want to live. It might seem shocking to some people but I think it would be an insult to you, Sarah, not to take the life you're given and do something with it. But this time it has been harder. I wasn't prepared for all these physical changes — I couldn't even hold the baby. I wasn't me in any way I could recognise.

In the ICU for two weeks, I had a lot of time to think; in hospital until May, I had even more thinking time. I woke up in a geriatric ward, not knowing what had happened. And do you know what else had happened, Sarah? They had cut my hair off again! The nurses had decided it was easier for them, to wash me and look after me, so, bang! Yet again, my lovely long hair had gone and I didn't recognise the woman in the mirror. In fact, it didn't even look like a woman in the mirror — I felt so . . . unfeminine.

I also had to reflect on how I had felt when I was left in a coma, paralysed down the left-hand side of my body. All I could think of was you. Was it time? Would I be reunited with you at last? I'm not sure I had the strength to decide, I think I was just going through the motions.

Until you decided for me.

You saved me, didn't you? You made the choice, my angel.

I was in such a dark place, not really knowing whether I'd live or not, or whether it was worth it. I hated that feeling, hated that I wasn't fighting every second, and I never thought I'd recover. When something finally woke inside me and I did decide to fight back again, I thought it had come from nowhere. Then I realised it was you. You were pushing me; you were telling me that I had to make the choice to live again because I'll always owe it to you. I need to keep striving forwards because so many innocent children like you are denied the precious moments of life. I couldn't just lie there and die, I couldn't be in the 50 per cent that didn't make it – I had to be one of the winners.

Despite the odds, I pulled through. And I know it was you – the doctors might disagree, but *we* know, don't we, darling? It's still so hard, though. I've got loss of movement, speech difficulties, memory loss, and I was warned that I wouldn't even be able to do really simple everyday tasks. To start with I didn't handle it at all well – I wasn't very good at being a 'disabled' person and I certainly found it hard to see how some people treated me differently. They only saw the limp, they only saw the stick; they didn't see *me*. I've become invisible; I've had to come to terms with the fact that I was so close to just not being here any more that I am vulnerable, that it could all end any second. You would think that I, of all people, would have learned that lesson all too well, but I thought I was invincible. It's scary that everything can be gone in a crack of a second, and that the others could have been facing a huge loss again. I have no idea how they would have coped.

I do wonder how much I'm to blame. I said to you last year that there were times when I knew I was doing too much and when I didn't feel very well. Did I cause this? Did I cause the stroke? I was so relentless before, I just kept pushing and pushing, never once thinking that I needed to sit back and take a rest: I had to fight for you all the time. This has made me realise that, if I don't sit back sometimes, there will be nothing left of me and the fight will have ended. I know that those achievements are yours too, but you need me to be your voice. I'm so proud of what you've achieved since you died, Sarah, but sometimes – and definitely since last December – I find it so hard when I realise you've now been gone longer than you were alive. That's a hard fact to wake up to every morning, so please forgive me if I was weak for a little while.

You're still such a part of me. The pain isn't as raw as it once was but that doesn't mean that it's bearable – it'll never be easy. There are times when it hits me in the face, when I just feel drained from the fact that you aren't here with us. So, I used to breathe through it, drink water, fiddle with my hair; focus on something else. Lying in the ICU, staying in hospital, there was no running away from the loss of you. I think the stroke did happen for a reason as it focused me, it reset my life. What a hard way to do it, though. In the space of one day our family had lost a mother and a partner. I woke up having had a stroke and the person that I had once been had disappeared overnight. Everyone thought that I should be grateful to be alive, but I wanted to do more than just breathe – I wanted to live, to move, to cook, to fold my own laundry – all the everyday things that I'd just taken for granted.

All I could do was concentrate on nothing but getting better, doing my exercises, going to physio. The stroke made me take a deeper breath than I ever had before and look at what was going on in my life. I had Mole and Lee and Luke and Charlotte and Ellie but I was running on empty; I was running myself into the ground. I needed to focus not on the things I didn't have or hadn't achieved, but what I did have and had managed. Some days were harder than others – some days I had to just be thankful I was still here rather than set the goal of climbing another mountain.

The thing is, when I finally did get home I felt like a visitor in my own home. I cried for three days, which isn't like me at all. Every time I heard the word 'stroke', I thought, *that's for all old people*. All I wanted was to sleep, because in that state I could still be the old me, could still walk without help, climb the stairs, make dinner, style my hair … everything that was now such a struggle. I just wanted the normal stuff back again. I needed a carer; I needed someone to teach me how to send an email. I would be in the middle of trying to make a cup of tea and couldn't remember why or how. I was so desperate that Ellie wouldn't be given the task of looking after me – she was so little, and I didn't want her only thoughts of me to be this woman who couldn't do anything. It's been such a frustrating time, Sarah, but I'm fighting back, I really am.

I was still in hospital when Levi Bellfield was charged with the murder of Milly Dowler ... Still in hospital when there was a General Election ... Still in hospital for the announcement of the extension of Sarah's Law later in August ... That was the hardest thing. I was in the breakfast room when I was told it was being rolled out nationally. There was a big hurrah about it but I almost didn't care: it was an anti-climax. How could I not feel something about that?

By the time I got home, I did see what a huge achievement it was but I was also distracted by the fact that Roy Whiting was appealing his sentence. I was there to watch it all, even if he wasn't. He was successful, I guess – it was reduced from fifty to forty years before parole. I was disappointed but I suppose I had always expected him to appeal against the sentence imposed by David Blunkett. The judge did stress that the sentence was imprisonment for life, and that Whiting would be detained 'unless and until the parole board is satisfied that he no longer presents a risk to the public. Even if the parole board decides then or at some time in the future to authorise his release, he will be on licence for the rest of his life.'

I had your brothers and sister with me when I was asked to speak outside the court. When I think back to the age they were when this all started, I can hardly believe it: Lee is now twenty-three, Luke is twenty-one, and Charlotte is fifteen. Ellie wasn't there, of course, but she wasn't even thought of when we first watched Whiting being tried. I told the world: 'The family is clearly disappointed that the tariff has been reduced, but he will be well into his eighties before he is eligible, so it's not a terrible, terrible thing, and could have been a lot worse, so we carry on as before. He's in prison now, he can't hurt any children there. I'll continue campaigning for a safer Britain for children.' And I meant it. It was important that the judge mentioned you just before he announced the new minimum term but it's stark when someone else does that, it hits me hard. He said, 'I invite everyone present in court, before we go about our daily business, to pause and for a moment remember Sarah Payne, who would now be eighteen if she had not been murdered, and reflect the grave loss her death has caused to her family and others who loved her.'

Ten years, Sarah, ten whole years we have been without you. The anniversary of losing you is always hard, but your birthday was even worse. An eighteenth birthday is such a special thing and you were never allowed to celebrate it.

★

It still makes me so mad that prisoners continue to have their battles funded by legal aid, when children like you aren't even allowed to blow out the candles on their cake. I still wanted what I have always wanted – a fairer system for victims and a system where they have as much access to legal aid as prisoners.

The world goes on and the fight goes on. Jim Gamble, who was chief executive of the Child Exploitation & Online Protection Centre (CEOP), has resigned in a row over its future, and the Home Office has just accepted this. There have been plans to assimilate CEOP into the National Crime Agency and Jim doesn't feel this is in the best interests of children and young people. I agree, and his resignation is a terrible thing. Jim changed the face of child protection for the better, forever, and I'll never forget that. He wanted to gain more independence for the agency rather than allow it to become part of a greater National Crime Agency; he feared the new moves would make the CEOP lose its identity and devalue its priorities. I'm actually disgusted with the government for betraying Jim Gamble. It was the worst possible news and a devastating blow for UK child protection. Phoenix put out a statement, which said: 'We cannot begin to describe how disgusted we are with our own government for betraying him and for betraying all of our children. This cannot be allowed to happen; we must stand up and fight, we must do what is right for the protection of our children against the crimes of paedophiles'.

The government didn't care, it seemed. Labour, the opposition, said that they would have given the CEOP the operational freedom it needed to become even more effective and they agreed that the government's plans will harm child safety networks.

It wasn't the only bad news.

The government has also decided to break up the Forensic Science Service (FSS). Roy Whiting would be free without its work, Sarah – this is something that matters. I was supported by dozens of leading forensic scientists who warned that the UK's justice system would take a backward step if the service closed. The Home Office said it was confident the move would not adversely affect the criminal justice system, but they are wrong – they are very wrong indeed. They claimed that the service makes an operating loss of £2 million a month, but the decision should not be guided by money. As a victims' advocate, I knew that 90 per cent of most current sex offender cases rely on forensic services to prove their cases. How could the government ignore this? But they could, and they did. These are bad decisions, my darling, and I feel that the fight has taken more than a few steps backwards just at a time when I am at my weakest.

I was trying to get back to work, but it was harder than ever. The short-term memory problems were horrendous and I'd been left with a lot of issues with my voice box too – for a while, it was really high and fast, as if I was on helium. While rehab was supportive at that time, my

PTSD was severe. I was having flashbacks, panic attacks
… everything was at the front of my head, being busy,
whereas I had always tried to push it away with work. I
wasn't sleeping and I had too much time to think. The
worst thing of all though was that my family was fractured
when I came out, and I needed to put that together. My
role has changed – I hate that, I hate them looking after
me. I've always had a very traditional relationship with
Mole (he works full-time and normally I cook and clean
and feed everyone and look after the kids) and that brings
challenges – he has to do the shopping and he isn't that
sort of man. These are new battles, princess, but the old
ones haven't disappeared.

I think this is the year I've finally realised that, although
you don't have a life, we must live ours. My body not
working makes life hard – physical difficulties are
something I've never experienced before. I've always
been very fit and healthy, I've always walked everywhere
as I never learnt to drive, but now I'm struggling with
coming to terms with being a disabled person and life has
changed for all of us. Stress and grief leave their marks,
and part of me is so very sorry for living, for not being
with you.

I work with Shy every day. We have a virtual office and
she reteaches me how to use the computer, one painstaking
step at a time. I swear the woman has super-patience! My
memory is shot to pieces and I forget as soon as I learn,
but she keeps going, keeps going over it again and again.

She is a blessing in my life, Sarah, and she will keep me strong. Everyone I love will keep me strong, including you. xx

2011

DEAREST SARAH —

A Royal Wedding — how you would have loved that! I've always been a fan of the Royal Family, and I can't help but think of how much you would have delighted in watching a real-life princess being made. The entire country was excited about Prince William marrying the beautiful Catherine Middleton, not to mention an extra Bank Holiday to help celebrate. Along with everyone else, I watched with immense pride and awe as the ceremony was televised. I missed you so much on that day, but of course Ellie and Charlotte were just as excited.

There are other developments that are even more exciting, though. Sarah's Law has been extended to all forty-three police forces in England and Wales. The

Metropolitan Police is the last force to join the scheme and, now that it has, I think I can finally say we have achieved a great thing. The police have admitted that your law has not led to vigilante attacks, despite what the opponents always said. The figures showed that we were right to fight for this – of the 878 enquiries to 24 police forces, 84 identified sex offenders and there were 110 cases where further action was taken, such as social services being alerted. One father told the BBC that without it, his family would have had no way of knowing a man linked to their child was not to be trusted. He said that he had looked for information from the police about a man who toured village fetes and festivals and had befriended his son, and they revealed the man had a conviction for sexually abusing a boy of a similar age. The man had offered to take the boy to festivals, and claimed he was a foster carer and teacher. 'It was as if he had thought in advance about the kind of things he would have to say,' the dad said – and he was absolutely right, because they do, they have it all worked out.

Levi Bellfield, a convicted double killer, was found guilty of Milly Dowler's murder this year and it has made people realise just how important the right legislation and checks are. No one will ever bring you or Milly, or Holly Wells or Jessica Chapman back, but we can try to stop there being any more cases like that, we can try and stop more shattered lives.

★

Just as I started to feel a little better, as I was making some – very slow – progress with life after the stroke, I was hit by more shocking news. There has been a huge scandal about journalists at the *News of the World* hacking private mobile numbers. I've only followed it a bit as my concentration isn't too good these days, but I've been told by Scotland Yard there is a chance my phone may have been one of those targeted. This isn't what I was told earlier, when the scandal first came to light. In fact, they had specifically said my name wasn't recorded in the notes of the journalist who is behind most of it. Now the officers say that they have found my personal details amongst his notes. I'm absolutely devastated and deeply disappointed at this disclosure. To think the paper has been behind me since the start – and now this? I was so sure that I was protected from it all that when the paper published their final edition in July 2011, I said they were all my good and trusted friends.

Now the police say that a mobile phone I was given by the paper is referred to in the notes they are looking at. The phone had been given to me some time ago so that people who supported the campaign for Sarah's Law could contact me easily – why would there be any other side to that? I've always been open with them; I've nothing to hide, so I can't quite come to terms with this. Rebekah [Brooks, as she had become on her marriage in 2009] is appalled too – she has said that the allegations are abhorrent and particularly upsetting because I am a dear friend.

I have to be honest, princess: I'm in bits about this. I don't even know whether they managed to hack anything, it's just the thought that they may have tried which disgusts me – I thought they were my friends, I thought they were my allies. Those were the people who came to Nanny's funeral, they came to Grandad's funeral; they visited me in hospital after the stroke. Did it mean nothing? I had believed them when they said I wasn't on the list – in fact, I had come out and spoken about it because they had behaved shamefully with regards to the Dowler family. It had been discovered that they had hacked and deleted messages on Milly Dowler's voicemail. I had been perfectly open about my anger regarding that – I wrote in that last farewell piece for the newspaper: 'We have all seen the news this week and the terrible things that have happened, and I have no wish to sweep it under the carpet. Indeed, there were rumours – which turned out to be untrue – that I and my fellow Phoenix charity chiefs had our phones hacked. But today is a day to reflect, to look back and remember the passing of an old friend, the *News of the World*.' And now? Now, I don't know up from down.

Rebekah [Brooks; she resigned as chief executive of News International in July 2011] has come out again in support of me – that means a lot. She said, 'The idea that anyone on the newspaper knew that Sara or the campaign team were targeted by Mr Mulcaire is unthinkable. The idea of her being targeted is beyond my comprehension.

It is imperative for Sara and the other victims of crime that these allegations are investigated and those culpable brought to justice.'

The Phoenix team have been working hard to get me through this, but I was so confused. My mind was foggy anyway because of the stroke, and I just wasn't as sharp as I needed to be. It was making me wonder about my relationship with Rebekah – all I could hold onto was that I was always open about things, and I think I'm a good judge of character. Our relationship had started more than ten years ago, a professional partnership which became a close friendship. Now, there was such a strain on it.

As I fought my way through the fog, I had to just cling to what I knew was true: it was Rebekah who had thrown the paper's weight behind the campaign. It was her paper who had helped with Sarah's Law, who had run the name-and-shame features, and who had tackled sex offenders more strongly than any other media outlet in this country had ever done. We were good friends, I knew – I just had to hold onto it. In an interview, Rebekah had reflected on how we first met, and I can remember it so clearly. She said, 'I took a chance and drove down to see Sarah's parents, Mike and Sara. The press pack waiting outside were more than a little surprised when I turned up on the doorstep. Inexplicably, Mike and Sara agreed to see me and the repercussions of that meeting started the Sarah's Law campaign.' That was the start of the million signatures campaign and the change of everything.

They had always helped us, Rebekah had always helped us. At no point had I felt things were running away. In those early days the *News of the World* team rang us on a daily basis to see if we wanted to stop or halt, or if we wanted to withdraw our support. The truth of the matter is, Sarah, they didn't need to target me: they could ring me up any time, day or night, and they did. I had no secrets from them – why would I? The only thing that I kept private was Mole, and they respected our privacy even though they knew about the relationship. They didn't need to hack me, and that is something I have to remember. They didn't need to, so I really doubt that they did.

The truth was, I felt a bit adrift now that the paper was no more. It had a massive impact on me as I had lots of friends there – it wasn't just a job for them, they were losing a part of themselves. They're not cold, it affects them. They are fantastic people and I'd never say a bad word about them, they always treated me with respect. Rebekah did help so much and I felt part of a team. It's the end of an era – I need to hold onto that.

I tried to look at it from another perspective. I suppose that I was very closely associated with them and so, in some ways, it could be seen as a bit of a relief as I could set my own agenda. Phoenix is my life's work now. I won't lose what I had with Rebekah – there is absolutely no proof that she did anything wrong with me, and I will hold onto that.

★

The after-effects of what happened aren't so obvious to everyone, darling. There are effects years later. People still want you so they can be more closed to Phoenix. I always try and see the next thing to do, so I just have to look at how I can move the love they had for you through the campaign to the next stage at the Trust. PTSD makes me break things down into chunks – I don't see a mountain, I see a step at a time, and it helps me deal with huge challenges.

Dad hasn't managed that, I'm sorry to say. He's been in terrible trouble his year and he's now in prison, darling. I have had so little contact with him. Around 2005 or 2006 he moved to Kent and cut himself off from us; he pretty much buried himself and I had to think of your brothers and sisters.

Now, all his problems have come together. He has admitted hitting his brother on the back of his head, arm and hand when they were both drunk. They had been bingeing on vodka and cider when it happened, and your dad ended up glassing Uncle Stephen.

The judge said that he had the 'deepest sympathy' but there had to be at least eight months served. The defence lawyer summed up what most of us were thinking when he said, 'The assorted aftermath had a life-changing effect on him and his then wife and his family. It's desperately sad. He never sought nor was offered assistance with bereavement counselling. It's just terribly sad in his of all cases that that advantage wasn't taken.'

And it's true.

It's all so sad, but your dad made choices and, as someone who believes that people have to accept the consequences when those choices are bad ones, I have also had to accept that this is the outcome. I hope it brings him to his senses, but I really do doubt it – he's too far down that path.

Now this very difficult year is coming to an end, I've thought again about what happened at the *News of the World*. I've got a bit of distance and the confusion and disappointment I felt earlier, when it all came out, has been tempered. I will always thank them from the bottom of my heart for everything they did for me and the children. We had some good times together. They would make the children smile even when they definitely didn't want to – they turned each meeting that I had to attend into something fun for the kids and they always asked their opinion too. We mattered to those people there and nothing will ever change my mind on that. They nurtured me through probably the worst eleven years of my life. We had invested in each other and I still say, to this day, it was them, Sarah and me who got Sarah's Law onto the statute books – there was collective blood, sweat and tears in it.

Now is the start of a new chapter, sweetheart – I'll find new allies if I have to, and I'll remember the old ones, but nothing will stop the fight. xx

2012

DEAR SARAH —

In February we celebrated the Queen's Diamond Jubilee, then in July, the Olympics came to London – but I had a wonderful celebration of my own when I was awarded an honorary doctorate by the Open University!

When I saw what they had written about me in the press release I was blown away.

Sara Payne, a highly regarded child-protection campaigner, victims' advocate and international bestselling author, has been honoured by The Open University for her exceptional contribution to public services. Inspired by personal tragedy, the death of her daughter Sarah, Sara launched a successful campaign to bring about the Child Sex Offender Disclosure

Scheme – known as Sarah's Law – which allows parents to
check the criminal records of known sex offenders. As a voluntary
Phoenix Chief Advocate, Sara has worked for over a decade
speaking for the victims of paedophile crimes who cannot speak
for themselves. She was appointed the first Victims' Champion
by the government in 2009, delivering the well-received report
Rape: The Victim Experience Review for the Ministry of Justice.
Sara has received many awards, including Most Inspirational,
Pride of Britain, Children's Champion and Woman of the Year,
and was made an MBE in 2009.

Was that all me, I wondered. Looking at it written down,
it seemed pretty damned impressive, even if I say so myself!
It meant so much to me – that report was pretty much
my doctorate anyway – I just hadn't been linked to a
university when I did it. To have my work recognised was
phenomenal. I knew that there was still a huge amount
more to be done to improve victim justice and recovery
rates, by challenging failing services and anti-victim
prejudice; developing victim support and helping educate
the advocates of the future, but this award would help me
a great deal as it would give me accreditation really.

I was actually embarrassed by it at first as I wasn't sure I
had earned it, but when I met the people who had chosen
me for such an amazing accolade, it turned out that many
students had used me and Sarah's Law as a topic for their
own theses and degree projects. The people at the Open
University decided that I should at least have the title they

felt I had earned, through such hard work, and hoped that I would use it with pride.

I had to go to Ealing Cathedral for the ceremony, where there is the longest nave in Britain. Me, with my wonky side not working properly, and a walking stick in one hand, a strange gown floating about me, and a desperate desire not to fall over! The last part was an achievement in itself.

When I came away from the ceremony, I was exhausted but I certainly wasn't embarrassed any more. I was determined and very proud to use my full title, so Dr Sara Payne MBE was born that day. I guess I'm sad that my parents didn't live to see these achievements. Mum could have boasted about it when she was in the corner shop or to her friends, and Dad would have grinned when he was down the pub – they would have loved it and been very happy. They had both been so proud of how I had handled myself since your death. I remember Mum once asking me how I had coped, because she herself had found it so hard to bury her son.

'That's simple, Mum,' I told her. 'It's because of you and everything you have taught and shown me.'

I talk to you all the time, darling, but I talk to them too and I am so grateful for the person they made me.

I sometimes look at other people in my position and I know that, actually, I'm one of the lucky ones. Winnie Johnson died this summer. She was the mother of Keith Bennett, who was killed by Ian Brady and Myra Hindley.

Brady has never revealed where Keith is buried and now Winnie has gone to her grave without being able to say goodbye to her child. She always said that it would be Brady's final sick twist to leave her without that knowledge, and she was right.

There have been plenty of occasions when Brady made Winnie think he was about to tell. Giving her hope seemed to be something he enjoyed, as she searched for her boy for almost fifty years.

Winnie's family don't believe she got the support from the police that she needed, support that I was always lucky enough to have. They say that Brady did reveal all in a letter but the police never looked for it, that they delayed matters which could have put Winnie's mind at rest.

Winnie spent so much of her life pleading in vain for Brady and Hindley to help her find Keith's body so that she could give him a Christian burial. He had been lured into their house when he was just twelve years old, walking to his granny's house, and never knowing the evil that was waiting for him. He was their third victim and they showed him no mercy, just like the others.

When Brady claimed there was a sealed envelope with all the details about Keith, only to be opened after his death, Winnie had a final spark of hope but there were delays in the police getting that information about the letter and then still more delays in taking any action. Her other son, Alan, is now hoping that he can find out what happened to his brother, but, to me, that just carries on the horror for that poor family.

Winnie had been to the Moors on many occasions – she had gone with TV teams, with psychics, with geologists, with the Army, and with spy satellite teams. Nothing uncovered Keith. She employed a private security firm and sniffer dogs to find him; she spent every penny she had, and still she died without an answer.

Winnie was a Christian, but she said in an interview before her death, 'I would like to tie Brady to a stake in the street and tear bits of flesh off him, to torture him as slowly and as completely as he has tortured me. And then when he was dead, I'd happily bang the nails into his coffin myself. A lost child is something which destroys part of you at the time and then the rest of you slowly. It can and does drive you mad.'

That way of thinking would indeed drive you mad, Sarah. Winnie had chosen the hymns for Keith's funeral and made plans for a horse-drawn procession. She even kept a cross on her mantelpiece for the event, and I think she gave her life to Brady and Hindley by doing all of that.

I'm not judging that poor woman at all, but people like Brady and men of that kind, they love to taunt us, they love to take as much as they can. I wish Winnie could have found peace, and I hope she is with Keith now, but when I looked at her, I always thought, *There but for the grace of God . . .*

It could have been me; it could so easily have been me.

I looked at her and thought I was one of the lucky ones. You were found, there was an inquest, there was prison – there were no unanswered questions really so I'm lucky. I had spoken to Winnie through the Victims of Crime Trust: she was a grieving mum who would have fought forever. I so hope he's found. Brady has that hold over her and her memory now; he has that forever.

I won't let Roy Whiting do that to me. My work is more important – *your* work. My final goal, darling, is that you are remembered more than your killer.

The year has ended darkly, Sarah, but I hope there will be some light from this eventually – the heads of the Jimmy Savile investigation have been announced. This whole situation has been proof for everyone that the rich and famous do it too, not that I've ever doubted that, I've heard too much. For years everyone had heard rumours and innuendo; it was no surprise but the scale and collusion were. I know how they do it, and Savile was a prime example: they fragment; they take one victim from each place. There were single voices until he died and then they were united. People were silenced and lost in the system. The charity work was a trade-off; he did it all to prevent being challenged. It has made people more willing to talk, I hope. Victims do tell, but people don't listen. And he did it all right under their noses and nobody stopped him. People don't see what they don't want to see, you have to start looking – I hope we all look harder now.

I just can't comprehend when people are so unsupportive of others trying to do good in the world. I had set up a Facebook page so that people could see what we were campaigning about, but I was constantly targeted by trolls. They have been writing vile messages and suggesting that sickening paedophiles know where our supporters live and are coming for their children.

One of them was a disgraced former teacher who has served time for downloading images of child abuse. It read: 'Paedogeddon – they are organised and they are coming for your kids!!!' This was from a man who had previously harassed me a great deal. He was nothing more than a bully. Men like him don't want campaigns like mine because as more victims are empowered, more paedophiles will have their dark secrets exposed.

The truth was, the campaign *was* working. More than 200 children had been protected from potential harm during the first year of the Child Sex Offender Disclosure Scheme, and over the last 12 months the police have received more than 1,600 enquiries and over 900 formal applications. At least 160 disclosures relating to child sex offences were made, together with at least 58 made concerning other offences. It was great news, but there always seems to be a downside to anything positive. Not long after the figures were released, a High Court ruling that sex offenders' human rights to privacy should be considered was made public. The ruling said that offenders should be given a say before their presence is disclosed and their human right to a family life should also be taken into account.

It disgusted me.

There was a test case brought by a repeat sex offender from the Sheffield area, where two judges agreed he had the right to make 'representations' to South Yorkshire police before local parents who made enquiries about him were told of his criminal past. The judge in charge of the ruling said that a 'balancing exercise' was needed between sex offenders' human rights to respect for their privacy and family lives on the one hand, and the interests of protecting children on the other.

Yet again, we were facing the battle between the rights of offenders and the rights of victims. When the judge said that criminal records and other information about sex offenders were often inaccurate, I wanted to scream, *then make sure they are accurate! Don't blame the victims, don't make life worse for them, don't put children at risk*. They were looking at the wrong problem.

People need to open their eyes, to see what is happening, and to find the courage to speak up when they know things are weighted in the wrong direction. Help me find the strength to help them, darling. xx

2013

HELLO PRINCESS —

Another family without any resolution is in my thoughts, darling. Mark Bridger has been found guilty but five-year-old April Jones's body is still not found. I met April's parents a few times when I was writing my column for *The Sun*. Oh, the pain of this case! It was all so sad, but so avoidable. That man is disgusting, and he was a convicted paedophile who should have been on the radar. When I met Coral and Paul Jones, I found it very difficult emotionally – I could see where they were on this journey. I was so cross that doctors were saying they were depressed and treating for such; clearly Coral is still in shock and extremely vulnerable

They're broken. You can call it anything you like, but I know that it's PTSD. Coral, to my mind, definitely has

PTSD and should be treated for that. It angers me that pills are handed out when clearly a person needs a whole lot more than that. They're asked to react in a certain way for others, not for themselves. Bridger's locked up safe and they're fighting, struggling every day. What do these men learn from each other? They'll be deemed safe one day and leave with better skills. It's scary and dark. I would make them work forever – the taxpayer shouldn't have to pay for their luxury and their legal bills.

I desperately hope that the horrific death of April will be the final straw that makes people realise this doesn't have to go on. There *are* things that can be done if we are strong enough to take action. It's time to say no more. One of the main actions that must be taken is for Internet service providers to take steps to stop horrific acts of child abuse being accessible to any sick pervert who looks for them. Mark Bridger was addicted to looking at these images online, minimised as child pornography, when we need to get across the fact that every single one of those images is that of a real child being abused in real life. We need to stop saying we can do nothing about it, that it's free speech – there are the resources and the technology to stop this. It will be difficult and it will raise some awkward questions about rights in a free society, but the rights of children should come above all else. Search engines can do so much for good; they must build on technology and do something about this.

When someone searches for an illegal site, they should

get a message from the search provider that is a warning. They should be warned that, if they go ahead, they will be reported, and then that should be followed up on. We already get warnings when some sites look unsafe, when money and personal details are involved —we must now do it for something much more precious.

If people are searching for adult pornography, there should be a 'safe search' option just as many mobile companies do —search engines should take this one. You should have to prove that you are an adult before you can access those images. The fact that many of them are images of real abuse and trafficked woman is another issue we must deal with, but when it comes to children, we need to use all the technology there is, and develop more of needs be so that the protection of the innocents is taken seriously. There is so much science that could be used, including identifying images and intercepting them by recognising their digital fingerprint; photo technology could be used, all sorts of things that would allow search engines to automatically seek out, identify, and locate known child abuse images. We need to start identifying search terms that mean an abuser is planning something of unlawful intent, and we need to fund the organisations that can help.

We need to save children, it's as simple as that.

I feel so strongly about child abuse images on the Internet because it has been proven so often that there are many Mark Bridges out there. He gorged on those sickening images, removing any barriers he may have had until they had disappeared, until he felt he had to go out and act on his sick desires.

There are proven links between paedophiles viewing child abuse images online and then committing sexual offences. That is why we have to act: they aren't sitting still, and we need to get off our backsides and do something. This issue should be at the top of the agenda for any party in power, no matter what their views on any other issue. I find it absolutely bewildering that it's not. How can anyone, politician or not, fail to see not only is this a huge problem, but it's one with a solution? You would think they would like that; you would think after all the rhetoric they spout, and all the things they *can't* change, they would grab the opportunity to actually do something. Why have successive governments not done something? Why do they not deem this worthy of their action?

I desperately hope that the anger felt about April Jones's death can galvanise some action. These killers are inhuman and we need to avoid being drawn into that anger for the sake of it, and move beyond how upset we are that another child has gone. We need to take those emotions and do something with them, something that will protect more children, every child. This is the best way to honour April's memory and to ensure that we stop having these terrible cases.

Mark Bridger's computer and phone were full of images of child sexual abuse. He had searched online, using terms that could leave no one in any doubt as to what he was after, but he wasn't charged with any crime in relation to that. Those images drove him to kill, and even the judge said he was a paedophile, but he wasn't convicted of anything like that. In some mad world, if he is ever released, Bridger wouldn't even be on a sex offenders register. Does it matter, people might ask. He's going to be in jail forever, they might say . . . But is he? We've seen plenty of killers appeal; we've seen plenty have their sentences reduced as our family knows only too well. There is already talk that, by calling Bridger a paedophile, the judge has undermined his human rights and that could give him grounds for an appeal too. It's absolutely disgusting but we can't sit back and just roll our eyes.

So, I met again with Coral Jones, a woman who is still in deep, deep shock over the loss of her beautiful child, and suggested we work together on this. 'If I can help save one child, I will be happy,' she told me. Her words all hit home: 'I have hit rock bottom and I've only just started coming back. But I want to do this for April, I want to do something in her name . . . There's no reason for these sites to be there. If you're looking at a paedophile site, then there's got to be something wrong with you. He put in words like "naked five-year-old" – there shouldn't be any results at all. There should be no images. We know he was searching these sites that day, that he looked, looked again, went out and suddenly there's little April. There was a direct link between what he looked for and what he did.'

Coral is absolutely right and no one should forget her words — when those search terms are put in, *there should be no results*. There should be no images that feed into the horrific appetites of these monsters. When Coral had to look at those images at Bridger's trial, she knew they would be forever burned in her mind — but why were they there in the first place? I told Coral that she was stronger than she thought, that she would get through this, but I'm not sure she believed me. In that dark place, the shadow world of loss and grief and PTSD, not much gets through.

At times I'm still in that world, my love. I'm not sure I'll ever leave it now — I know its geography, I know the ups and downs. We're heading towards another summer. Another July. Those are hard days, Sarah. I sometimes feel that I'm watching other people experience summer, because for me it's one of the worst times of the year. I see children laughing and playing and then suddenly, I'm jolted back to reality. I find myself worried about their safety, desperately hoping they get home, back into the arms of their loving parents and families. In the thirteen years since you have been gone, the loss of you hasn't lessened. I may seem to have got over it, I do laugh and I'm happy at times, but the loss is still there and always will be. I miss your voice and your smile; I miss your laughter and your innocence. I miss how kind you were and how open to the world you were. That hasn't changed.

I can't get past the memories, darling. I don't want to get past the good ones, but when I'm flooded with those I don't want, life just feels so heavy. The flashbacks seem almost constant – they either come through or I'm fighting to keep them away. Either way, it's hard work, to say the least. I just need to get through every summer. Not to make things easier, but to make it less raw. There are flashbacks all the other times too, of course there are, but they don't have the weight of that anniversary, horrific though they are.

You would have turned twenty-two this year, my sweet girl, but to the world you're always eight. What would you have been like? A mother? You would have still been caring, I know that, always looking out for people who were lonely or bullied or shy. You are still looking after the lost ones, aren't you? But I so wish we were doing it here, rather than the way it is. I try to keep positive and to only think of you with love and light, but the darkness creeps in, just as it does for all of us mothers who have one less child to hold.

We're a gang that no one wants to be a member of. When I look at Coral Jones or Kate McCann, or any of the others, I know that we each understand what the other is going through, but I know we all have our individual pain too. For Denise Bulger, the news that Jon Venables, one of the killers of James, will be released again is horrendous – she must be going through absolute hell. Twenty years have passed but she will still be in agony every day; we all are. And still the perpetrators appeal, still they think they are the victims. It's laughable, really. To hear the recent news that George St Angeli, a convicted paedophile, has become the first to have his name taken off the Sex Offenders Register in a landmark court ruling – and that nearly fifty other sex offenders are applying to have the same thing done – makes me feel disgusted. It undoes a lot of work I have toiled so hard and long on, but they won't beat me; they'll never beat me.

They've tried to take so much that was precious from me, but they couldn't take the inspiration or the love. We can do this, princess. xx

2014

HELLO SWEETHEART —

I've had to close my Twitter account, darling. There are some horrible people out there. I've had years of abuse and unrelenting harassment online; I've been stalked and harassed by paedophiles and the abuse has been disgusting. I sometimes wonder what the reaction to your death would have been if social media had been around when you were taken. So much potential for good, and so many chances for people to connect positively – but there are always those who ruin things. Would I have been told I was a bad mother? That it was all my fault? Without a doubt. Look at how the McCanns have been treated – without people being able to post anonymous hatred at them, they would never have had to fight the double battle of losing their child and being hate figures too.

Shy made the announcement for me, saying that trolls 'have caused so much distress @DrSaraPayne has been forced to close down her twitter account'. Many of the abusive tweets were about you, babe. How can people think those things, never mind make the leap to typing them out and posting them? It has happened a lot since I hit the public eye, but back then it was mostly mail in the post. I did receive a lot – some nice, some not so nice – but since social media has been more prolific, I have had more than my fair share of haters. They seem to go with the territory, to be honest. For the most part, I try to ignore them but there comes a point when it just gets too much and I need to get away from them, so, this year I made the decision to close my account. It was important that neither I nor my supporters had to see it all, or indeed feel like they had to fight my battles or defend me as they often did. The haters will say anything just to get a rise out of people, because, for them, any attention is better than none – they don't get any from me so they become more outrageous. They would say things like 'Roy Whiting is innocent', that the whole thing was set up by me, that I am a professional victim (whatever that is). I can assure anyone that I would swap my life now for a moment with you, Sarah, for a chance to say 'goodbye', a chance not to leave you that day, but people think I've made millions from the press, that I'm glorying in a lavish lifestyle. Nothing could be further from the truth. In fact, I have point-blank refused money in order to move Sarah's Law forward to keep both the integrity of the campaign and my own reputation in one piece. I would rather starve than have anyone be able to say that of me or my family, or the campaign

I suppose the hatred makes me focus on the things I can change. Recovering from the stroke is still very hard indeed, but I think I have accepted it. I am more positive when there are physical limitations I can fight; that's easier than the invisible ones. When I was first in rehab, I gave myself a year as that seemed such a long time. I soon realised I was wrong. Complete recovery is something I will never achieve, I know that. I get tired of fighting – for change, for things not to happen. I have seen a sea change in sex offenders, and adult survivors, but not enough. Occasionally I wonder how much more I'll have to fight.

I wonder other things too. Would you have been strong enough if you had come back? If you'd come home after a few days with him? What a life you would have had – there's only so much a person can take. So many people are hurt forever by the things done to them. I'm emotionally damaged forever, so how on earth would you have coped? Half my body doesn't work and I fear the next thing will floor me. I try not to dwell but I'm scared of another aneurysm because there's only so much a person can take, so much they can be battered.

★

It seems that the universe disagrees; it seems the universe thinks I can indeed take more.

Sarah, how can I say this? Sugar coating is no use. I've never hidden things from my children that they need to know, and you definitely need to know this.

Sarah, your father isn't with us any longer. He's gone. It was all, finally, too much for him.

It was all such a shock. I got a call around midnight from Nanny to say 'he has passed.'

'What are you saying?' I asked her.

'Just that,' she replied. 'Michael has passed.'

I didn't know what to say. It was the alcohol, Sarah – I hadn't realised his drinking had got so bad. All I could think of was my children.

I called Lee first as he was on holiday with his family, bless him.

'Lee, you need to come home,' I told him after I had delivered the shocking news. 'Your brother and sisters are going to need you.'

I waited until morning to tell the others and anyone else who needed to know. I don't think they could believe that I was delivering more death news – I could hardly believe it myself. I'm surprised anyone ever answers the phone to me really – I'm such a bringer of doom.

I do feel that I need a break from all of this, but it's never going to happen, is it?

Is it OK if I talk to Dad for a little bit, babe? You can

listen – I want you to listen – but I just need to tell him a few things.

I want to remember the good things, Mike. I don't want my mind to just be filled with the times it was wrong, the times it was toxic. I want to write this down so that Sarah knows, so that they all know that there was a time when we loved each other very much.

I remember when we were so young, so innocent; when all we wanted was to be together to raise a family and make a home. Those days and nights when we spoke of our future, not our past.

I remember when we only had eyes for each other. We went out, we had friends, we had good times, but we would catch sight of each other across a crowded room and smile, knowing that we were together, knowing that it was good.

I remember when we laughed all the time. At silly things, at things we had done and places we had been and people we knew. We didn't want the world, we didn't want riches or fame – we just wanted to be surrounded by love. I remember that you were amazed by how I had been brought up, by the love my parents had for me and by the values they had given me. They welcomed you because we were together and we both hoped that we could be like them.

I remember talking about what we would name our children when they came – and our shock when that day arrived so much sooner than we thought it would. I remember their births, Lee and Luke and Charlotte, and how we gazed at them while they slept, marvelling that we had created these perfect people.

I remember when we had Sarah and we knew, from the

beginning, that she was different, that she was an old soul, someone who was too gentle for this world. We indulged her love of fairies and magic, we called her our princess, and we thought we could keep her safe forever.

I remember that it was different with Ellie, but she was still meant to be, and that you loved her as you loved all of your children.

I remember when we went through those terrible times when Sarah was taken and you found it so hard to be public, but you never stopped me from doing what I needed to do. You knew that there was something to fight for, and although being so public made you uncomfortable, I'll never forget that you were there beside me, at the press conferences, at the appeals, even though you hated it.

I remember the times you squeezed my hands or looked at me a certain way and we knew, we just knew, that this would probably break us but we needed to be there, together, for as long as we could manage.

I remember that you didn't question me leaving the door open for Sarah, or setting her a place at the table, or buying gifts for her, or keeping all of her things. I don't know if you would have done it differently, but you supported me when I wanted to do it my way, and I thank you for that.

I thank you for them all, Mike. No matter what went on between us, no matter what we did to each other, there was love, wasn't there? And we showed that by making these wonderful people. They will do you proud, all of them, all five of them, and they will always remember you. I'll remember you too, Mike — I hope you're at peace now. xx

2015

DEAR SARAH —

We placed a statue for you at your school — something simple, just a memorial of a girl, a girl who happened to look a lot like you, but a girl who would stay there, a girl who would never leave. Except for some people, that was too much to ask for. The statue has been stolen, princess — you've been taken again. You never seem to stay. How could anyone do that? How could anyone take that memory of you?

There was no plaque beside it. In fact, no one other than a few members of the PTA and the school staff even knew what it was. To the rest of the world it was just a girl. We had to be so careful when it was put in place. The children at the primary school were so little that I didn't want them to be forced into trying to understand something that was too big for them, I didn't want them to be scared. Besides, you had left that school two years before you were taken so the children there didn't have a memory of you. That's why we did it quietly and gently – and now that has all been ripped apart again. I wonder when there will ever be any peace, Sarah.

Despite this, I do feel as if I'm finding myself again. It's been six years since the stroke, but honestly, that's nothing. It's such a huge thing to happen to any person or to any family, and, although it sometimes feels as if it was yesterday, it wasn't – and that hits me at time. I have lost chunks of my own memory, and to be honest, sometimes I don't even know what's gone on as I can't remember it in the first place! Really I can only laugh at how ridiculous it is.

I think things are getting better this year, though. I've started to see just how lucky I am and how much more needs to be done in terms of fighting for what matters. Two years ago, we all had to deal with the shocking news that Shy's son, Ayden [Keenan], had committed suicide. He was such a lovely boy, a gentle soul who was bullied mercilessly for being gay. When he decided that he just couldn't take it any more, at only fourteen, I think it made us all pause to think. The loss of such a young boy, so loved and so special, has hit home more this year than any other. When it first happened, Shy suggested that we start a campaign on bullying and that we contact *The Sun* to see if they would be interested in a column. I think they were on our side because they knew it was such a major issue, and they themselves were seeing a huge rise in the number of stories appearing in which terribly young children just couldn't go on any more.

Shy and I started talking to parents whose children had been in those awful situations and it opened my eyes, Sarah. Do you know we met some whose five-year-olds had taken their own lives? What sort of a world do we live in where that happens? So many of these children are living in absolute despair. I feel very strongly that the rules which exist within school need to exist outside the school gates too – all of the training and all of the awareness that is levelled at pupils, then, for some reason, as soon as the bell goes they forget all of that. Some of them bully and attack and insult those they see as different, and it's as if none of what they learned applies. Bullying should always be reported to the authorities – it's far too major a topic not to be taken seriously. Children are dying … I'll never stand for that. However, it has made me think that I have also given in to the bullies. Leaving social media, hiding from online trolls – who are those people if not bullies? Their school gate might look a little different, but they're the same inadequates, the same type who hide behind words that they think will never hold them to account. Well, I wasn't made to hide, princess. I've always taken people on, and I'm ready to do that again.

Ayden's death has hit me harder this year than it did

when it actually happened, I think. I've finally had that wake-up call, and realised that I'm the same warrior I've always was. My body might be a little slower, and my brain may take a little longer to catch up, but I'm getting there. I supported Shy when her son died, and I'll keep on supporting her; part of that will be through taking people on wherever they are. The people who think it's OK to talk about sexual abuse in terms of attacking the victims, calling girls slags, making consent into something it's not – I'm not going to sit silently while they are the ones shouting. It's time for me to shout again too. And I want to shout this at them – *don't you dare!* Don't you dare think you can get away with this, because I'm back, and I'm watching you.

So, I'm back on the campaigning trail, with Shy by my side, and we're pretty much indestructible. It has given my brain a boost to start thinking this way again, I feel. I fight well for other people – I was a lioness when Shy was broken, and I'm ready to start being that way again for others too.

I'll take myself on where I need to as well. I'll fight this stroke every step of the way, because I think I've been sitting back, feeling a bit sorry for myself, losing the real Sara. Now, I do feel more like how I was before the stroke, before you left even. More of the old me is here again. I think being physically damaged has taught me a lot of things. I've had to allow people to help me and in itself that has been very hard – I was always the one who did everything for everyone, and it's just not in my nature to be otherwise. However, I want my life back and I won't get it unless I fight. I want my energy, my health, and I really want my laughter to return. There has been the odd moment, but I want to enjoy *all* of my life, not just moments of it.

Finally, something good has come of social media. We all took to Facebook, to Twitter, to everything we could think of, all of the family. We made your statue too hot to handle and whoever took it ran scared. They dumped it in the garden of a woman who knew someone who was Facebook friends with Lee and so we have it back. We have you back, my darling. I actually think the idiots who took it were unaware of what it even represented until we went so public. No one in this area would really do anything to hurt you or your siblings, I know that in my heart; I think they didn't realise the magnitude of what they had done and then they panicked. This area suffered so very much when you went missing and I don't think it has ever fully healed. Now that the statue has been returned, I think we can all see that – it was a lesson that needed to be learned. We are a community still hurting from the loss of you, but we are also a community that will never forget you, and a statue isn't the real memory that lives on in the hearts of the local people.

I think this whole experience showed me something too – and that was that social media could be a force for good.

I hate to think I was running scared at any point, that just isn't me at all, so the strength I have found from the people rallying round us with the stolen statue has shown me that I need to take the good when I find it. Ignore the haters, ignore the trolls; I can't do anything about their choices. The things they say are a reflection of their inadequacies. They are hiding behind a computer screen, tough because they are hidden. They wouldn't dare say these things to my face and that's the difference between us. If we did meet, I'd happily take them on – I would argue and I would prove to them the power of knowing that you are trying to do some good in the world. I bet they'd run a mile, so why on earth should I worry about them at all?

No, I need to keep my energy for what matters. I know that social media would probably have changed the law quicker back in the days of your campaign, but it would have dragged me down. I did get sacks of letters every day for such a long time, but a lot of it was very dark and the police screened it all. Of course I was lucky it happened that way; they couldn't have protected me in the same way now, some of it would have slipped through and who knows how that might have affected me? I don't think I would have survived in the same way. I was always brought up to see the good in people, but I think that approach to life would have been stretched back then. Could I have dealt with the case, the campaign, and the hatred that invisible trolls would have dished out to me? Probably, because I know I can deal with anything really, but my

God, it would have been an even harder fight. I wonder if they think of that? I wonder if they are truly trying to break people? Do they think they're untouchable? They shouldn't think that because the tide will turn, and there will come a day when all of that hatred which is spewed out from all of those keyboards will finally be challenged. Who knows the real extent of the damage it has done in the meantime, though? Who knows how many Aydens there really are? How many teenagers, or even younger, have had one text too many, one post that finally pushes them over the edge and makes them feel life just isn't worth living any longer? It's truly shameful.

When I first had the stroke, everyone commented on how young I was — it was awful that I'd had one at my age, but great in some ways, because it gave me such an opportunity to 'get better'. But I knew nothing — I thought I'd be fixed in six months, I thought it only happened to old people. Now I know that you're probably never 'fixed' and that it can happen to anyone, even children, even babies. I did have a good range of movement, they told me, but it took a while for it to sink in that, actually, after a stroke, that can still mean you're limited years later, decades even. Doctors told me that there was no reason for my body *not* to work; everything was in place for it to resolve itself. But it didn't — my left side didn't 'resolve'. For a while they had no idea why things weren't connecting, why my brain and body weren't talking to each other. They spoke of more operations and often I was back in A&E with debilitating headaches. Then, one day, they did a CAT scan and showed me the results. Mole and I sat there as I saw a picture that proved exactly why so little communication was taking place: a third of my brain was completely black, it just didn't work. To see it there, literally in black and white, was shocking. It was visual proof that I was a different person.

I took stock for a little while and then Shy and I started looking around for someone, somewhere; anything that could help. We searched high and low, but I'm not sure I knew what I was looking for. I had put on so much weight and I felt completely unfeminine – I just didn't feel like a woman any more. No one had ever spoken to me about that side of things. I had womanly feelings, I had a partner, but I felt like a useless lump. It dawned on me that this was linked to my previous notion of stroke as an old person's condition. They don't bother about looking pretty, do they? They don't want to be sexy – and that was the dilemma. Just as I had put all stroke victims together as one mass, now I was putting myself in that category.

That couldn't go on.

So we searched, and we found an answer: a tiny company in Yorkshire called Shapemaster came to the rescue. Exercise was to be the key to all of this. They gave me an exercise chair that plugs in and moves my body for me when I myself can't. It builds up my muscle tone and I can finally see a difference, Sarah – I can finally take ownership of my body again. My hair has started growing and I've learned to do my make-up one-handed. I have also discovered online shopping, much to the amusement of your brothers and sisters, who claim I'm an addict! Almost as soon as I started exercising, I also started to stand up straighter. I felt better and people said I looked better. It all had a knock-on effect. I was so used to people saying that I looked tired, or 'not myself' that it was a welcome relief to have positive words; it made me even more determined to do this, to make myself me again. I guess I was a trailblazer for Shapemaster and they certainly saw the improvements very quickly. They couldn't see some of it, though – they couldn't see how much the exercise was helping my brain, helping with my depression. In rehab, I'd given myself a year. I had been told that was completely unrealistic and I thought I knew better, but I was wrong: my own deadline passed and I was nowhere near 'better'. I missed the little things like being able to clap when my grandchildren did something, to cheer them all on, to get down on my hands and knees to play. I was young for a grandparent, but I'd have been as much use if I were a hundred years old.

This has been the year that I have finally accepted that I need help with being so down. I went to my GP and was offered CBT, which proved to be a fantastic help in making me feel positive. I think I was always a naturally positive person but life had changed me, the stroke probably most of all. I'd stopped doing my hair or caring how I looked or what I wore, and the therapist made me notice all of that. Part of it was grief, but part of it was depression too. One day I burst into tears when I was chatting to the GP – I remember him being very new and he hadn't known me for very long. He was aghast that I hadn't been offered therapy after you were taken, princess, and put me on antidepressants straight away. To be honest, I had very little faith in that decision and although it was a slow process, they helped a lot. Everything started to come together: I saw the GP, I started antidepressants, I began CBT, and I exercised. It wasn't easy but the alternative was much worse. I would tell anyone to see their GP if they feel low – they really won't judge and they really can help. Also, I think it's up to all of us to do what we can, so I cut out caffeine, I pretty much stopped drinking, and I looked at myself again as a person.

I think all mums could use to do that.

As your children get older, they don't need you so much, certainly not in an active way. You're put on a shelf, really. They might still need you emotionally, but physically, you're in a rut. I certainly was. So, I started working with The Stroke Society. I was back to having meetings in Downing Street, and I was meeting people who were in a much worse position than me. Few people think of those who have strokes while they are still young, but it happens a lot. The problem is when you're written off, it's all too easy to simply give up, so I wanted to give people a bit of hope. You think a stroke is just about one side of your body not working properly, but it alters everything, including your approach to life, even your sense of humour. I'm much blunter these days and I can be disengaged. I feel my mind drift off in the middle of conversations but my memory is getting a little better.

It's time to reintroduce me to the world – I'm not just a grieving mother, not just a campaigner, not just any one thing, I'm me. I've woken up properly this year. Six years is nothing in the lifetime of a stroke, and maybe fifteen years is nothing in the grand scheme of things.

I've also stopped making lists. Well, that's not strictly true – I've changed the type of list I make. Instead of having lots of things 'to do', I write down what I've done, what I've achieved. You feel miserable at the end of the day if you just have bullet points saying what you haven't managed, but if you have a list of what has been done, that's completely different. It's about turning the negative into a positive.

It always is, darling, it always is.

All of this has made me realise that this is the perfect time to tell the rest of your story, *our* story. I have so much in my head that I have said to you over the years, but it is as if I need to get it all down in the way I want you to hear. I don't just want people to get confirmation of what they *think* they know about me, I want them to know it all. I want them to be able to hear the conversations I've had with you, read the things I've told you, and realise that, even when the person you love leaves, the love stays. I want them to see that, even if they feel lost, there is still hope – you can cope, you can survive, you can *live*. Even when you think there is nothing to make you ever want to wake up in the morning ever again, there is, there will be. There will be sunshine, there will be laughter … It will be a different life, but it is still life, and that is all we can hold onto.

You don't fall down just because bad stuff happens. Life is for living, and good stuff can happen too. The fog will lift. It will come back, but the gaps in between will get longer, slightly easier. It will never disappear, you never forget, but you do learn how to carry your burden in a way that makes it all a little more bearable. Prepare for the bad days because they will be back at some point, but build yourself up with love and laughter and joy whenever you can because, at the end of the day, what else is there? How else can we all get through this? You might have to wait a while, you might break even more as the years pass, but it's still worth it. It's worth it for the ones who had it all taken away.

Living is a privilege. We both know that, don't we, princess? xx

2016

PRINCESS —

I live an honest life with my children, I don't hide things from them as you know all too well, but there are some aspects of my life that I haven't spoken of – not really, not to you. For so long, I drank so much. I drank to forget – to feel alive, to feel numb. I drank because I couldn't cope, and because I needed to show I could; I drank because it made me feel better … Or worse, I wasn't sure. Did you know that about your mother? I don't have an off switch when it comes to alcohol, and that needed to stop. After what had happened with your dad, I couldn't go down the same route. My children couldn't lose another parent that way, I couldn't repeat his mistakes. So, this year, I've stopped living like that. The stroke has made me realise that I'm not invincible. I needed to take control of my own life rather than just try to fix everyone else's, I needed to concentrate on eating properly and exercising, looking after my own body.

I had a little breakdown at the start of this year (isn't it funny how we describe things to ourselves when we don't really want to unpack what has happened?), and I've had to concentrate on my mental health as much as my physical health. My GP has been wonderful and I've done a course of CBT, which has helped me find ways to cope when the darkness gets too much. It does get too much sometimes, darling, but I'm hoping I can start to find little bits of light again.

I was shocked when the darkness came. You cope for a while then it hits you out of the blue again and you're back where you started. I think we all need to just learn that it's OK to ask for help, it's OK to say you're not coping, that you have to keep on trying until you get the right person. Finally, I took my own advice and did exactly that, but I had to say that things were awful – an admission that took a lot. Everything came crashing down this year so I had to take a step back and ask myself why. Or maybe it was more a case of 'why now?' I keep going, Sarah, I always do, but the stroke took so much energy from me and I just didn't seem to have the same coping strategies any more. Do you remember when I told you that I had developed this way of slicing myself up into different Saras so that I could cope in the early days? Well, this is the year that I've found that, for some things, there isn't the right slice of me there to cope. There wasn't a Sara who could just sail through a stroke as if nothing had happened.

I'd never faced anything like this before — it was a battle for me, and me alone, really. All of the old fights had been won and I'd been left almost a soldier without a war; then, out of nowhere, there was a new battle. I wasn't prepared for it and it has actually taken me a while to realise how much I've been drained.

The thing no one talks about, Sarah, is how much a stroke steals from you as a woman: I just didn't feel attractive any more. I was still young, only in my forties, and yet I felt done, exhausted and old. I felt that no one would ever be able to see past my disability — and, finally, after all that had happened, I was too tired to care. Sometimes I feel as if the world knows everything about me. I've been so public since 2000, but after the stroke, it changed. It was something that was done behind the closed doors of hospitals, or at home; no one was signing a petition for me, no one was marching in the streets for stroke survivors. I'm still a woman, still a person — and I need to make sure no one, including me, ever loses sight of that.

It's time to concentrate on the good, my love. When I think back, I can see it; I remember all of the children that have been helped and all the children who will be helped in the future. So many people have contacted me about Sarah's Law and told me that it has made a difference, and that won't stop. I always say making an application to try and find out about someone doesn't necessarily mean that you'll get that information – many more applications are done that go nowhere – but when it does, you can make the right decision for you and your family. I have had so many parents tell me that everything fell into place once they had the disclosure, and I remind them that their gut instinct is there for a reason. They'd all had niggly feelings about someone, but the disclosure had given them proof that they were right to think or feel that way. What happens if nothing comes up? Well, that's great! You'd never forgive yourself if it was the opposite way round – if you said nothing, did nothing, and there was something there. Remember, it's better to lose a friend than to pick up the devastated pieces of a life.

I always say, Sarah, if Mum or Dad lets someone in (a gardener, a group leader, a new friend, anyone), then to a child, that makes that person safe in their eyes. Mum or Dad have said they're OK simply by allowing them access to the little world of that family. If that person has acquired that access for bad reasons, the child is left wondering what on earth they can do – how can they speak out, how can they tell? Mum or Dad would be disappointed, surely? Would they even believe the child? That is why it is up to the adults, and Sarah's Law allows them to change their actions based on *proof*. It isn't down to niggly feelings or gut instinct any more – it's down to knowing that this person has a history of something or other. I'll admit sometimes the history might be a different one, but it generally shows that the individual is hiding something, and do you want someone like that around your precious child?

The world doesn't have to be a bad place, but we can make it safer – make sure you're the good person; make sure your child is surrounded by people who love them in the right way. I know that some people want to bury their heads in the sand but we can't afford to do that with child abuse. It *is* a huge problem, no one knows that more than me, but do you know something else? Big problems always seem big. That's why we have to break it all down into manageable chunks. It's the old joke about 'how do you eat an elephant?' and the answer being 'one bite at a time'. We can only eradicate child abuse by all doing our best, one person at a time, making the world of each child safer, one at a time.

Sometimes we have to start with the child inside us. We have to go back, deal with the PTSD, deal with what is still hurting our emotional health, and make a better present day. I firmly believe that we should have no shame or embarrassment about emotional and mental health, and that everyone should ask for help when they need it. Start with your GP, they are your first port of call, and if you don't get on with them, just try another one – keep trying, keep pushing, until you get what you need. I've had to pull on every resource I have to try and get better, and you'll have to do that too if you're in the same boat. It may take a village to raise a child, but it also takes a village to maintain a healthy, balanced adult – ask for what you need to be that adult, or be part of the village for other people. Never forget that people are good. They want to help; they want to do something. Even people who are scared about anything to do with mental health issues – those are the ones who will be happy to do practical things for you. Not everyone will hold your hand while you're in a dark place, but the ones who won't are usually happy to make you a cup of tea! It's so important not to try and cope so well that you don't ask for help – you'll just sink deeper, you'll just fall further.

Funnily enough, this is all part of the fight against child abuse too. You can show your children how to talk, and how to talk honestly, by doing it yourself. Talk openly. Be genuine. It's all connected. If you're not comfortable with someone being around your child, speak out about that too. Do something. Don't sit there silently worrying – who knows what's going on while you don't take action? Yes, it might be uncomfortable to raise issues, it might lose you a 'friend', but do we really, ever, want to trade temporary adult discomfort for the safety of a child?

For the past seventeen years I have done nothing but fight – and that's fine. I couldn't save you, but I have saved others, and that will never end. It's what I'm here for. But I need to stay, I need to stay healthy and well so that I can keep fighting, so that is why I've really concentrated on my health this year. I'm even getting more of a reaction from the left-hand side of my body; not movement as such, but definitely something. A start. I have noticed that my PTSD calms down a lot when I eat more healthily, when I don't drink, and when I exercise. I'm learning to listen to my own body. I'm avoiding processed food and cooking from scratch; I'm concentrating on mindful eating and losing weight. It's all about taking control without becoming a control freak – like most things in life, I guess. I keep the anxiety bearable by doing breathing exercises and making sure I sleep well. And, as I've always said, I take medication when I have to because there's nothing shameful in that. No one should judge another person for what they need to do to survive, and there is no shame in taking medical help when it is offered or you ask for it. I'm not ashamed of my depression or my anxiety or my PTSD. On the contrary, I own them – they aren't me, but they are a part of me.

There are so many similarities between how we discuss child abuse and how we discuss mental or emotional health issues. The discomfort ... The silence ... It's time to break down all of those barriers and stop thinking that keeping quiet helps anything.

I do feel that this has been a long journey, a very long journey indeed, princess. My body has been through enough – but I'm listening now and helping it repair. I'll always fight for the next thing and my body needs to be just as strong as my mind. So, what is that 'next thing'? It's Anti-Victim Prejudice, or AVP, and I feel that it is the key to so much of what has been done in your name. I've always thought, *no wonder kids don't talk, given how we talk about them*, and it's that awareness that's behind AVP. When a child is abused, we speak about whether they deserved it, whether they asked for it. No child ever deserves it, no child ever asks for it. We talk about their behaviour rather than the behaviour of the perpetrator. We lay as much blame as possible at the door of the victim, and hide away from the uncomfortable truth – the truth being that we'd rather blame a child, sometimes even a baby, than look at what we encourage in our society. That has to stop.

I can see glimpses of the woman I was again, and I welcome that so very much. I still want to do things; I still want to fight. One day, I might cycle to Paris. One day, I might do a naked photoshoot. One day ... one day ...

I know these things:

I love and I am loved.

I'm in a good place.

I look forward to my future, whatever it is.

I will always move forward; I will always try to change the world.

And I have the best warrior in the world beside me – so let's do it, Sarah, let's move some more mountains, my darling girl. Your stubborn, dedicated, and finally happy, mum. xx

2017

MY DEAR, DARLING, BEAUTIFUL SWEET PRINCESS —

What can I say now that we are approaching the end of this journey?

Thank you.

That's the main thing – thank you.

I love and miss you every day and that will never change. I'm so proud of what we have achieved together. I guess if you had still been here, then it wouldn't have happened this way. However, it is what it is. I believe that you have saved so many children from horrible existences, given them the courage to say 'no', the courage to tell, and you have also helped this whole country to learn a lesson they needed to learn so very desperately.

I'm so lucky to have had you in my life and will always

wonder why fate put you with me. Do you remember when I said I always thought you wouldn't be with me forever? It's true – I never thought I'd see you as a grown woman, and I never will. But I was wrong when I thought you wouldn't always be with me, because you will. You are with me every day, every moment. When I think I can't go on, when I cry – but also when I laugh and when I love life . . . there you are, beside me, laughing and loving too.

Our family has changed so much, but time would have done a lot of that anyway. Lee and Luke are men now – and fine ones at that. I like to believe that they do well because you watch over them. When I see them now, at the age they are, it shocks me to think that I was that young when I lost you: I was a mother, I was a wife, but I knew so little. The learning has been hard-won, but I think that was always my path to follow.

Charlotte has grown into the most beautiful young woman. She has the voice of an angel, but I wish you could send her the confidence to believe in herself. If the world could hear it, if the world could recognise her talent, then I think she would finally throw off the mantle of 'just' being the sister of Sarah Payne. She'll get there; she has a strength that lies within all of our family that will take her to exactly where she needs to be. And I have no doubt that you will be there with her, singing as she sings, proud as punch of the little sister who never left your side.

Little Ellie is the image of you and Charlotte put together but she carves her own way through life and I think she always will. She has her own challenges to deal with, but that child has had an independence inside her since the day she was born. It will take her far and it will leave all of us amazed at what she will achieve. The world needs to watch out for that one!

When Ian Brady died in the early summer of this year, there was – naturally – an outpouring of public bile for him. It's understandable, but I would rather think of those who were lost, not just to him and Hindley directly, but to the families who were left behind and ripped apart by their actions. I thought of poor Winnie Johnson, who went to her grave never knowing where her boy Keith Bennett was buried. I thought, not of Brady taking that secret with him, but of Winnie, hopefully reunited with her child. I don't want to spend another second thinking of those who create the heartache, I want to give my thoughts and my energy to those whose lives were broken. Not everyone can move on, not everyone can find their peace, and there should certainly be no pressure or expectation that any bereaved parent should do those things, but I'm not sure I would have survived if I had given anything away that wasn't love. I had to keep the love going and I had to keep the fight strong. I don't wish hellfire on Brady, as I don't want to spend a moment's energy on him. I send Winnie and Keith and all the others my love and my promise – I won't stop fighting, and it will always be on the right side.

It doesn't mean that everything's perfect – I would still rather have you. I'm doing OK – I struggle sometimes without you but then I imagine you watching me and I realise how lucky I've been to have you at all. Your voice is always there and it's given me a voice too. That makes me lucky, not cursed. I hope I can always make you proud even when I make mistakes. I wonder what you would have become. I know this world is a little less shiny without you and it should mourn that loss. We should mourn the loss of every child – we should mourn the loss of their potential, the fact that we will never know or appreciate the achievements, discoveries, or differences they could have made. I just hope those children are all somewhere together, taking care of each other and watching over those that you loved and who loved you.

I often feel you around, Sarah. I swear sometimes I hear you giggle. And I hope I do – I hope that is what I hear. I wish with all my heart that you laugh every day.

Shine, my little princess.

Always be my rainbow – guide me through grey skies and make me remember that the sun will come out again because this, this is who I am.

I love you always and forever – Mummy xxx

Mole's story

I've always been in the shadows, really. People know that Sara and I are together, people who know us, but I've never wanted the limelight. I've always managed to stay private, even in public. The truth is, because I'm a bit of a Jason Statham lookalike (alright, maybe more Phil Mitchell!), when we are together at events or functions, there is often an assumption that I'm her minder. I don't bother correcting anyone, I'm happy just to let them think that.

But it's time for me to come out of the shadows, I think . . . and the only reason I would ever do that is to tell the world about the woman I'm proud to share my life with.

Sara and I have been together for thirteen years, since Ellie was only six months old, but we've known each other for much longer. We weren't much more than kids when we had a couple of summers where we spent all our time together. I wouldn't say we were in love back then, it was more like a crush, but when I think of all that has happened since, it's enough to make even an old cynic like me wonder about fate. We went our separate ways for a while – a long while, long enough for us to get married to different people. I moved away for a bit and was never really around too much as I was working as a lorry driver, but one day when I'd gone back to the area we had both known, I was sitting in my living room, watching TV. She walked past the window and, as she just slipped out of my line of vision, a flash of recognition hit me. 'I know her,' I thought to myself, but nothing else came.

The next day, the same thing happened at the same time (Sara was working in a different pub and on her way home when she passed). Again, I thought, 'I know her . . . don't I?' and then I answered myself. 'Yes! Yes, you do – it's Sara Williams.'

That's who she was to me. I didn't know her married name, didn't know anything about her life then, so she was still Sara Williams from all those summers ago. We got chatting a bit over the next while, but just as passing acquaintances. Sometimes I'd see her and Mike with the kids, in the pub for a family meal, or just as I was driving by.

When little Sarah first went missing, it didn't click. I still thought of Sara as Sara Williams – I hadn't even registered her married name, so my reaction was that of most people: it wasn't someone I knew. It was terrible and I felt for the family, but it was two days before I realised. When I switched on my TV and saw a press conference, rather than listening to the news on the radio in my lorry, it took a moment to sink in.

Mole's story

That mother, that woman whose world was falling apart as she begged the whole country to find her daughter, was the girl who had stolen my heart all those years ago. It touched me on a personal level, of course it did, but I'm not one of those people who jumps on bandwagons or has a breakdown when something happens to a celebrity they don't even know. I keep myself to myself, really. If someone asks for my help, I'll gladly give it, but I'm not someone who would think their feelings on something mattered more than the people who were directly affected. I watched the news and I saw people who were grieving – I don't mean the Paynes, I mean people who had never even known little Sarah. I couldn't help but think some of them were rubberneckers, some of them were following the story as if it was a soap opera, but that's just how I look at the world. I do judge, I do see a darker side sometimes, and I don't have the good heart that I now know Sara does.

As time went on, we kept in touch – it could be weeks at a time and then one of us would text the other, but we were comfortable in our friendship. She was going through such horrors, and I'd be listening to them, removed, on the radio in the lorry, often forgetting that she was the Sara I knew. The strength of her shone through from day one, and I was starting to realise that she meant a great deal to me. It was as if we knew each other, but we didn't. We had a past, but we didn't really know the people we had become. It was more than a friendship, but less than an affair.

Something had to give, and we finally realised that we had to be together. Sara had separated from Mike, and I left my wife. I'm not really one to believe in destiny, but then I think, well, it might have taken us over twenty years, but we got there in the end.

From that moment on, we've been a team. That doesn't mean that we agree on everything. Our views on paedophiles and the treatment of them couldn't be more different. I think that, when you find them, you should execute them there and then: they're never going to change. Get rid of them or lock them up and throw away the key – and, to be honest, if you're going to do the latter, why bother? Save yourself and the country some money, and do us all a favour by exterminating the scum. I have no compassion for them, but before I began my life with Sara, I'd never really thought about them before.

Like many people back then, there was an awareness that child sexual abuse existed, but it was hidden, unspoken – a secret, really. Sara brought it all out into the light for everyone. She shone a torch into corners most of us didn't even want to acknowledge. It was a rude awakening to me. I guess I'd been floating through life. My own childhood had been so different – I was part of a generation who got kicked out at nine in the morning during summer holidays and was only expected to come back when it was dark. As long as you were there for your lunch and tea, the only thing you had to do was stay out of your mother's hair. Of course there were perverts then, but we had no idea, not really. Sara made me face up to the fact that they're everywhere and it's mind-blowing. The fact is, if you abuse a child, get caught and go to prison for it in our society, you're actually very unlucky. Most of them get away with it.

Mole's story

Sara is very much against the death penalty whereas I think they're vermin – I have zero tolerance for anyone who abuses kids. I know that's vengeful of me, but I think a lot of people feel the same way. I'm in awe of Sara's goodness and her absolute belief that the good guys will win. It might take a while, but they'll get there. She is so resilient. I often say if they cloned her, they could skim something off and coat tanks with it. She's the most remarkable person I've ever known.

Of course she has her dark times but she is amazing. Life is unfair and she knows bad things happen – knows it more than most – but she just gets on with it. With Sarah's Law, everyone told her that she'd never get it passed, but her attitude was, 'Well, it might take me a while, but I'll get there.' And she did. I'd never seen anything like it. She would listen to everyone, nod, take it all in, and then, instead of getting annoyed, she would work out every possible argument and counter-argument. By the next time she met the person or the agency or the politician, she would have predicted everything they could have come up with. The other person always runs out of answers or setbacks before Sara does. She's sensible and thoughtful and she'll take on any fight – you'd always want her in your corner.

If I was asked what I wanted for her, if there was something I could give her, of course I would say happiness, but I know there's not really anything I can do. I can't give her Sarah back; I can't change anything. I can't reverse the stroke. That's been the hardest thing for me to watch and I wish, more than anything, for a miracle in medical science so that she could get her arm back. Before the stroke, we had quite a good life, really. I would think that some people may find that hard to believe because, for them, she'll be stuck in their minds as the woman from the press conferences, the grieving mother, the heartbroken campaigner. But we had our own life – we were the centre of everything. Parties, BBQs, wakes, a constant open house … that was us, and she deserved it. After the stroke, it all vanished. People disappeared; people who had loved what we had provided just weren't there any longer. I was left to cope, largely with two girls who weren't mine and who were questioning what on earth would happen to them if their mum died. The truth was, I didn't know. If I hadn't got Sara back, I have no idea what would have happened. When she did come back, for a while, I didn't really know how much of her there was. I think there are three versions of the woman I love – the old Sara, stroke Sara, and new Sara. I see most of them every day.

Life is frustrating for her in so many ways now – there is still so much she wants to achieve, but her body betrays her, her memory lets her down. She's still feisty, still involved; she's a mother, she's still very loving, but she gets so exasperated by how the stroke has affected her. What I want people to know about her is that what you see is what you get. It doesn't matter who she's taking to – the Lord Chief Justice or a single mum on a council estate who's worried about who might be moving in next door – she's the same Sara. Things happen, life changes you, but she still has that same core of *her*. She could have become a drug addict or an alcoholic, she might have run up huge debts or thought she was better than anyone else given who she was mixing with – but she didn't.

Mole's story

Through all the tragedy and the angst, she's the same person. That amazes me. She could bear resentment or hatred, she could be so many negative things, but she is just her. And *just her* is the most incredible woman I've ever met.

The only thing that surprises me about her is that she puts up with me. Despite everything, if she could she'd still move mountains. She'd still put her cape on and try to make everything better for children, for anyone who doesn't have a voice. And I know, in my heart of hearts, that she will . . .

One day, I'll come home, the cape will be gone, and there will be a note to say, '*Back soon . . . just off to change the world*'.

Acknowledgements

I'm dedicating this book to all those who have managed to stay with me while I've been on this rollercoaster. Thank you so much, Jenny, Shy (you never leave even when I break yet another laptop), and Del (for constantly fixing them). For Mole, who has pushed me so much and never settled for letting me settle!

For my gorgeous children – Lee, Luke, Charlotte, Emily, and little Ellie – and my four grandchildren, Charlie, Alfie, Tommy and Sienna. You are my world, my reason for being; my reason for getting up in the morning.

For my lovelies: Sam, Katie, Sarah, and, of course, you, Ali (keep the light on in the dark).

At John Blake Publishing Toby Buchan has been a constant support. His kind and wise words have helped when things have been difficult, and his input is much appreciated. I would also like to thank all of the people at John Blake who I don't know in person, but who have worked tirelessly to put my story in your hands. And to Linda Watson-Brown, who has helped me put it all down and gather it all together.

Many of these people never knew Sarah, but they have all added something to the fight to keep her memory alive, to make her a symbol of hope. For that, and for every single person who has taken the time to read my story, I give my thanks. Sarah would too — and I hope that, in her name, you will all never forget what is important here.

Let's make this world safe for children, for the people who matter most. Let's make this world safe because it's what Sarah would have wanted.

Appendix: If you need help...

With Shy Keenan, I have set up an organisation called The Phoenix Post. If you visit us at our website, www. thephoenixpost.com, you will find lots of information which will help. The main focus of our work is Anti-Victim Prejudice, or AVP. Our mission is to advocate for a better understanding of AVP, to promote good Emotional Health Services and work in the development and delivery of drug-free civilian PTSD management tools.

In the year that Sarah was abducted and murdered, Shy helped to trigger 'Operation Phoenix', a Merseyside police investigation/conviction of a paedophile network that abused many children (one of those children had been Shy herself). Shy had already set up and was voluntarily running 'Phoenix Survivors' to help those affected by 'Operation Phoenix 2000' and I was campaigning for Sarah's Law – in our separate work, both of us were challenging the socially groomed systemic AVP that all those victimised by paedophile crimes face.

In 2003, we set up the Phoenix Chief Advocates Group to fight even harder regarding AVP. The name was changed to respectfully acknowledge the fact that not all those victimised by paedophile crimes survive them. Working separately and together, but always in support of each other, I focused on challenging the paedophile's taxpayer/government funded secret keeping culture that was/is putting so many children's lives at risk, while Shy put her focus into outlawing the institutional systemic or AVP that has its foot so firmly on the throat of child protection that it can't actually properly protect children.

Working together with the government (across all parties), the authorities (across the whole child protection system), the media, and with the unprecedented support of the British public, I spearheaded the successful campaign for Sarah's Law, as Shy set about making incredible strides across the whole of the child protection/social system changing hearts and minds about the insidious, institutional and victim silencing AVP. We have continually worked together to change AVP laws and policies, challenge bad child protection practice, victim injustice or failing victim support/recovery and compensation services, while constantly striving to get the victims' voice heard on the issues that matter to them, without the prejudice. Having worked together for many years now, we have become multi-award winning, respected, and trusted voices.

Our advocacy services are, and will always be, free to those we advocate for all ages, genders, cultures, faiths and ethnicities

– across all of the UK. By 2012, we started to build The Phoenix Post, a community group to advocate for those victimised by paedophile crimes and the AVP that goes with that, and to promote better Emotional Health Services for those with Civilian PTSD. We were joined by the amazing Disability Rights advocate, Terrijayne Butler. Now a fully independent and registered not-for-profit company, we are working so very hard to spread the word about the dangers of AVP and PTSD. I believe very strongly that both can kill, and both need to be tackled at every level of our society.

We teach virtual seminars from our headquarters to address both, feeling that the virtual approach is perfect given that the 'real' world disadvantages and excludes those with disabilities at every turn. In the virtual world we have complete mobility and full access to everything that is often closed off to us in real life. We are now moving over to our Phoenix VHQ which marks the start of a brand new, far more animated chapter in our journey and working to develop the Phoenix PTSD house and garden 360 App and a virtual-reality game.

I hope you will join us there – Sara, xx